# 1001 Quips & Quotes for Business Speeches

## Richard S. Zera

*Illustrated by Myron Miller*

 Sterling Publishing Co., Inc.   New York

*Dedicated to my editor,*
*my conscience, my best friend,*
*my love, and my wife, Marinda,*
*and the three greatest gifts*
*God could bestow,*
*Jason, Tammi, and Russell.*

**Library of Congress Cataloging-in-Publication Data**

Zera, Richard S.
    1001 Quips & Quotes for Business Speeches / Richard S. Zera;
illustrated by Myron Miller.
        p.      cm.
    Includes index.
    ISBN 0-8069-8486-4
    1. Public speaking. 2. Wit and humor. 3. Business communication.
    4. Anecdotes. I. Miller, Myron, 1948–    . II. Title.   III. Title: Business
quips and quotes.
    PN4193.I5Z47    1992
    808.5′1—dc20                                               91-40120
                                                                    CIP

Quips and quotes from the *Reader's Digest* are gratefully reprinted with the permission of the Reader's Digest Association, Inc. All material © Reader's Digest Assn., Inc.

Quips and quotes from Douglas B. Smith's *Ever Wonder Why?* are gratefully reprinted with permission of the author. All material originally published by Ballantine
Books. Paperback edition published by Fawcett Gold Medal Books, © 1992.

10   9   8   7   6   5   4   3   2   1

Published in 1992 by Sterling Publishing Company, Inc.
387 Park Avenue South, New York, N.Y. 10016
© 1992 by Richard S. Zera
Distributed in Canada by Sterling Publishing
% Canadian Manda Group, P.O. Box 920, Station U
Toronto, Ontario, Canada M8Z 5P9
Distributed in Great Britain and Europe by Cassell PLC
Villiers House, 41/47 Strand, London WC2N 5JE, England
Distributed in Australia by Capricorn Link Ltd.
P.O. Box 665, Lane Cove, NSW 2066
*Manufactured in the United States of America*
*All rights reserved*

Sterling ISBN 0-8069-8486-4

# CONTENTS

# FOREWORD

As a frequent public speaker, and consequently a critical judge of other public speakers, I am a great believer in the importance of "spicing up" a talk with interesting stories or quotes. It is important that any quote or story have a purpose in a talk—whether to amplify or illustrate a point, or perhaps just to ensure the audience has an easy way to retain the essence of the talk. They may not remember all of the points you expound on in your formal text, but they probably will remember the stories you used to drive those points home. While some items included are of a very serious nature, others are lighthearted. The humorous items included are in the vein suggested by William Davis, who said, "The kind of humor I like is the kind that makes me laugh for five seconds and think for ten minutes."

I began collecting potentially useful items over the years for my personal use. Since my public speaking included college courses I taught, professional business seminars for various industries, many school and church organizations, and a variety of conferences and conventions, the nature of the quotes and stories kept expanding. As this file grew in size and diversity, it became an indispensable tool when I was preparing a talk.

When I couldn't find an appropriate quote to amplify a point a year ago, I spent some time in libraries and bookstores trying to find books that might help. To my dismay, I found either very large and often dated books that required many hours of reading in order to find something relevant, or books that included items so obscure or profound in nature that they were not practical for most verbal presentations. In short, it became evident that my own private collection appeared still to be the best source available.

It is with this background that I have attempted to compile a book that I feel will better serve the needs of today's public speakers. Rather than trying to impress the reader with the size of the collection, I have tried instead to be very selective. I have carefully selected quotes and stories that I feel have the best impact and utility. Obviously, my personal judgment was the guiding light in this selection process, but critiques of manuscripts of this book by colleagues in a variety of professions seem to support this judgment.

It is unfortunate that in some cases, the items I have used do not include a specific source. The nature of the compilation process—one that encompassed many years of jotting notes from other speakers, newspapers, magazines, and books—did not always afford a source. Numerous colleagues and acquaintances also began sending me little stories or quotes they picked up, usually without a specific source. Nonetheless, I wish to acknowledge the contributions of the authors and speakers who may have first said or reported the items included, even if they must remain anonymous. As Mark Twain said, "What a good thing Adam had—when he said a good thing, he knew nobody had said it before."

This book is intended to serve two audiences. First, as a practical and useful reference work, it can be invaluable to public speakers, including the business person who makes occasional presentations. It should also be of great use to those who speak more often, such as ministers, attorneys, teachers, and leaders of church, school, or civic organizations. I urge those using this book in preparing talks to familiarize themselves with the entire collection. It is quite possible that although the indexing process may have placed a quote in one category, it may fit equally well in others. Further, many items can have their emphasis changed to suit an entirely different purpose by simply changing a word or adding an introductory comment to serve as a bridge to the topic of the talk.

Second, the general reader should find this book quite interesting. Persons of any walk or stage of life can enjoy wit and wisdom in a form that can briefly and ingeniously express a thought or idea. Whether it's a humorous story or a poignant quote, the epigrams and witticisms included can be both enjoyable and meaningful.

# ACKNOWLEDGMENTS

First and most important, I would like to acknowledge the inspiration, love, and support provided by my wife, Marinda, and three children, Jason, Tammi, and Russell.

I would like to express my appreciation to Dr. Richard L. Conrad and Dr. J. Christopher Dalton of Bowling Green State University for their support in the compilation of this book.

In addition, to the dozens of faculty, staff, and friends who took the time to scribble down and send notes on interesting stories or quotes, many thanks. For serving as spiritual guide in this endeavor, warmest thanks to Father Thomas Leyland.

Special thanks go to Ron Zera for 25 years' worth of phone calls whenever he heard a cute story. In addition, the support and encouragement of a big brother has always been invaluable. For both of us, posthumous thanks to our parents for their love and commitment to our education.

Finally, since I have collected these quotes, anecdotes, and sayings over a period of years, without always noting or even knowing the names of the works, if any, in which they may have appeared, it is sometimes impractical to provide an accurate acknowledgment of the original source. Therefore, many thanks to all who contributed, even if some must remain anonymous.

## Ability

Never stand begging for that which you have the power to earn.

## Accounting

A financial secretary appended this note to her final annual report: "I wish to express my appreciation for the opportunity of serving as financial secretary for the past five years. I have truly received much more than I have given."

An accountant is a man hired to explain that you didn't make the money you did.

Old accountants never die; they just lose their balance.

# Adulthood

When I grow up I want to be a little boy.
—*Joseph Heller*, Catch-22

The four stages of man are infancy, childhood, adolescence, and obsolescence.
—*Art Linkletter*, A Child's Garden of Misinformation

# Adversity

By trying, we can easily learn to endure adversity—another man's, I mean. —*Mark Twain (1835–1910)*

Tough times never last, but tough people do.
—*Robert Schuller (1926—    )*

The difficulties of life are intended to make us better, not bitter.

Constant success shows us but one side of the world; adversity brings out the reverse of the picture.
—*Charles Colton (1780?–1832)*

Where the willingness is great, the difficulties cannot be great.
—*Niccolo Machiavelli (1469–1527)*

# Advice

Most of us only ask for advice when we know the answer but want a different one.

Advice is like snow; the softer it falls, the longer it dwells upon, and the deeper it sinks into, the mind.
—*Samuel Taylor Coleridge (1772–1834)*

I have found the best way to give advice to your children is to find out what they want and then advise them to do it.
—*Harry S Truman (1884–1972)*

Advice from an old carpenter: Measure twice and saw once.

9

To profit from good advice requires as much wisdom as to give it.

When we ask for advice, we are usually looking for an accomplice.

No vice is so bad as advice.

No man's advice is entirely worthless. Even a watch that won't run is right twice a day.

Good example has twice the value of good advice.

## Age

You know you're getting older when . . .
   The gleam in your eyes is from the sun hitting your bifocals.
   Your little black book has all names ending in M.D.
   You get winded playing chess.
   You're still chasing the opposite sex, but you can't remember why.
   You know all the answers, but nobody asks the questions.
   You sit in a rocking chair and can't make it go.
   Your knees buckle but your belt won't.
   You regret all those mistakes resisting temptation.
   You get exercise acting as pallbearer for your friends who exercise.
   You sink your teeth into a steak and they stay there.

Maturity: acting your age instead of your urge.

Everyone has talent at age 25. The difficulty is to have it at 50.
                              —*Edgar Degas (1834–1917)*

Anybody who can still do at 60 what he was doing at 20 wasn't doing much at 20.

You know you're old when you discover that your children are learning in history class what you studied in current events.

You know you're getting old when you start riding a bike and your kids take the car.

By the time a man can read a woman like a book, he's too old to start a library.

Middle age is when you wish you could have some of the naps you refused to take as a kid.

I am an old man and have known a great many troubles, but most of them never really happened.

—*Mark Twain (1835–1910)*

None are so old as those who have outlived enthusiasm.

Old age is like a plane flying through a storm. Once you're aboard, there's nothing you can do.

—*Golda Meir (1898–1978), former Prime Minister of Israel*

I'm saving that rocker for the day when I feel as old as I really am.                    —*Dwight D. Eisenhower (1890–1969)*

11

Growing old is not upsetting; being *perceived* as old is.

If you are 35 years old, you have about 1¼ billion seconds left in your life (1.25 Giga seconds in IBM terms). If you plan to retire at age 65, you only have about 216 million seconds left at your office desk. . . . Use them wisely.

My saintly grandmother was reflecting on her advanced years, and noted, "One of the things it is hardest to accept at my age is that most of my friends have already died." Reflecting on the sadness of her thoughts, I glanced up and saw a smile cross her lips as she quietly added, "But then, so have my enemies."

## Ambition

Woodrow Wilson, not often noted for his humor, was Governor of New Jersey before becoming President. One night, he was awakened in the middle of the night by a telephone call from a young civil servant. The young man blurted out, "I'm sorry to wake you at this time, but your State Auditor has just died. While I'm sure we are all saddened by this news, I would like to know if I can take his place."

Governor Wilson thought it over for a moment, then replied dryly, "Well, I guess it's all right with me, if it's all right with the undertaker."

We cannot do everything at once, but we can do something at once.

Don't let life discourage you; everyone who got where he is had to begin where he was.

When you are aspiring to the highest place, it is honorable to reach the second or even the third rank.

—*Cicero (106–43 B.C.)*

I think we consider too much the good luck of the early bird, and not enough of the bad luck of the early worm.

—*Franklin D. Roosevelt (1882–1945)*

## Anger

How much more grievous are the consequences of anger than the causes of it. —*Marcus Aurelius (A.D. 121–180)*

When we are right we can afford to keep our tempers. When we are wrong, we can't afford not to.

He who can suppress a moment's anger may prevent a day of sorrow.

If you are sensible, you will control your temper. When someone wrongs you, it is a great virtue to ignore it.

—*Proverbs 19:11*

13

# Atheism

An atheist's most embarrassing moment is when he feels profoundly thankful for something, but can't think of anyone to thank for it.

An atheist is a man who has no invisible means of support.
—*Bishop Fulton J. Sheen (1895–1979)*

An atheist is a man who watches a Notre Dame–Southern Methodist University football game and doesn't care who wins.
—*Dwight D. Eisenhower (1890–1969)*

# Attitude

One of the great mysteries and discoveries is that a human being can alter his life by altering his attitude.

# Banking

A banker is a man who lends you an umbrella when the weather is fair, and takes it away from you when it rains.

# Brevity

The Ten Commandments contain 297 words. The Bill of Rights is stated in 463 words. Lincoln's Gettysburg Address contains 266 words. A recent Federal directive to regulate the price of cabbage contains 26,911 words.

Talking or writing that is too long is generally the result of thinking that wasn't long enough.

All too many speakers condense a ten-minute talk into a one-hour lecture.

Let thy speech be short, comprehending much in few words.
—*Ecclesiastes 32:17*

Recipe for good speeches: Add shortening.

He can compress the most words into the smallest ideas of any man I ever met.     *—Abraham Lincoln (1809–1865)*

Brevity is not only the soul of wit, but the soul of making one's self agreeable, and of getting on with people, and indeed of everything that makes life worth living.

*—Samuel Butler (1835–1902)*

## Business

A company in which anything goes will ultimately be a company in which nothing goes.

At the time of the last walk on the moon, a reporter asked one of the astronauts if he had been nervous while strapped in his seat before being launched into space. "Well," said the astronaut, "of course I was. Who wouldn't be? There I was, sitting on a phenomenally complex rocket assembly with 9,999 parts all of which had to work perfectly—and each and every one of those parts was made by the lowest bidder!"

It is not the employer who pays wages—he only handles the money. It is the product that pays wages.

—*Henry Ford (1863–1947)*

Sign posted on closed gasoline station: WE UNDERSOLD EVERYONE.

A company is known by the people it keeps.

There are currently 21 trillion pages of paper stored in file drawers across the U.S. In a typical work day, U.S. businesses generate 600 million pages of computer output, 235 million photocopies, and 76 million letters. Combined, these documents are multiplying at an annual rate of 20–22%. The amount of stored information is doubling every four years. It costs approximately 25 cents annually to retain a paper document on file.

—*J. Raymond Sutcliffe, V.P., General Manager of Business, Systems Division of Eastman Kodak Co.* (Infosystems)

# Change

Everything changes but change itself.

—*John F. Kennedy (1917–1963)*

Consider how hard it is to change yourself and you'll understand what little chance you have trying to change others.

Great spirits have always encountered violent opposition from mediocre minds.    —*Albert Einstein (1879–1955)*

16

# Character

Character is that which reveals moral purpose, exposing the class of things a man chooses or avoids.
*—Aristotle (384–322 B.C.)*

Character is made by what you stand for; reputation by what you fall for.

Every human being is intended to have a character of his own; to be what no other is, and to do what no other can do.
*—William Channing (1780–1842)*

Ability will enable a man to get to the top, but character is the only thing that keeps him from falling off.

Good character is more to be praised than outstanding talent. Most talents are, to some extent, a gift. Good character, by contrast, is not given to us. We have to build it piece by piece— by thought, choice, courage and determination.—*John Luther*

# Children/Childhood

Children are like sponges. They absorb all your strength and leave you limp. But give them a squeeze and you get it all back.

"Mother," said Billy, "Bobby broke a window."
   "How did he do it?" asked mother.
   "I threw a rock at him and he ducked."

If you think kids today don't know the value of money, try giving one a nickel.

My young son had heard me talk about my job and the people I worked with for most of his scant years. One day, in order to let him see what the business world was really like, I decided to take him to my office. I introduced him to many of my co-workers, but he seemed unimpressed. I tried to amuse him with games on my microcomputer, but he seemed disinterested. As we drove home, I was perplexed at his lack of enthusiasm throughout the day and the sullen look on his face as he sat beside me in the car. I couldn't see the reason for his disappointment until he complained, "I never got to see the clowns you said you worked with."

Childhood is that wonderful time when all you need to do to lose weight is bathe.

Modern psychology tells us that it's bad to be an orphan, terrible to be an only child, damaging to be the youngest, crushing to be in the middle, and taxing to be the oldest. There seems no way out, except to be born an adult.

"We live in a decadent age. Young people no longer respect their parents. They are rude and impatient. They inhabit taverns and have no self-control."

—*Inscription on a 6,000-year-old Egyptian tomb*

18

A child's mind is like a bank—whatever you put in, you get back in ten years, with interest.          —*Frederic Wertham*

Not all the motives of the young are what they may appear to be on the surface. Take the very nice little boy in his Boy Scout uniform who helped a nun across the street. He was very solicitous, guiding her carefully through traffic, and gave her a smart Boy Scout salute when they got to the other side. "Thank you very much, young man," the nun said.

"Oh, that's all right," said the Scout, "Any friend of Batman's is a friend of mine."

The little boy was caught by his teacher saying a forbidden four-letter word. "Jimmy," she said, "you shouldn't use that word. Where did you hear it?"

"My mommy said it," the child responded.

"Well, that doesn't matter," the teacher explained. "You don't even know what it means."

"I do too," Jimmy corrected. "It means the car won't start."

Children have more need of models than of critics.

—*Joseph Joubert (1754–1824)*

A little girl came running into the kitchen, crying loudly, "Mommy, Mike broke my dolly!"

"Oh, what a shame," consoled the mother, "how did he do it?"

The child wailed, "He wouldn't give me any of his candy so I hit him over the head with it."

If children grew up according to early indications, we should have nothing but geniuses.

—*Johann Wolfgang von Goethe (1749–1832)*

The quickest way for a parent to get a child's attention is to sit down and look comfortable.

# Christianity

I believe in Christianity as I believe that the sun has risen. Not only because I see it, but because I see everything by it.

—*C. S. Lewis (1898–1963)*

If Christians would really live the teachings of Christ, as found in the Bible, all of India would be Christian today.

—*Mohandas Gandhi (1869–1948)*

People in general are equally horrified at hearing the Christian religion doubted, and at seeing it practiced.

—*Samuel Butler (1835–1902)*

No cloud can overshadow a true Christian, but his faith will discern a rainbow in it.    —*Bishop Horne (1780–1862)*

The Christian doctrine has not been tried and found wanting. It has been found difficult and not tried.

—*G. K. Chesterton (1874–1936)*

An ethical man is a Christian holding four aces.

—*Mark Twain (1835–1910)*


# Church

The church must be reminded that it is not the master or the servant of the state, but rather the conscience of the state.

—*Martin Luther King, Jr. (1929–1968)*

The most beautiful sight from the pulpit is a whole family seated together in a pew. The church service is not a convention to which a family should send a delegate.

—*Charles Myers*, Houston Times

If absence makes the heart grow fonder, then a lot of folks sure must love the church.

# Committees

On May 21, 1927, a secretary burst into the office of a Detroit executive and cried, "Mr. Murphy, a man has just flown from New York to Paris all by himself!" When he continued to work calmly, she cried out, "You don't understand! A man has just flown the Atlantic ALL BY HIMSELF!"

Now, Murphy looked up. "All by himself, a man can do anything," he said quietly. "When a committee flies the Atlantic, let me know."

A committee is a group of the unfit, appointed by the unwilling, to do the unnecessary.

Never has so little been so done by so many.

To get the job done, an ideal committee should consist of three people—two of whom are absent.

First, I want to thank the people who made this meeting necessary. —*Yogi Berra (1925–    )*

If the members of some committees were laid end to end, it might help.

Meeting: I came, I saw, I concurred.

A traveler stopped to observe the curious behavior of a farmer who was plowing his field. A single mule hitched to the plow was wearing blinders, and the farmer was yelling, "Giddyap, Pete! Giddyap, Herb! Giddyap, Ol' Bill! Giddyap, Jeb!"

After watching for a while, the traveler finally asked, "Say, mister—how many names does that mule have?"

"Just one, his name is Pete."

"Then why do you call out Herb, Bill, and the rest?"

"It's like this," explained the farmer. "If Ol' Pete knew he was doing all this work alone, I couldn't make him do it. But if he thinks he's got three other mules workin' alongside of him, he does the whole job all by himself."

"What a marvelous idea!" exclaimed the traveler. And when he got back to his corporate office in New York, he invented the committee.

—*Charles R. Edwards, quoted in* Reader's Digest. *Reprinted with permission from the November 1989* Reader's Digest. *Copyright © 1989 by The Reader's Digest Assn., Inc.*

We always carry out by committee anything which any of us alone would be too reasonable to persist.

—*Frank Moore Colby (1865–1925)*

Committee work is like a soft chair—easy to get into but hard to get out of.

A conference is a gathering of important people who singly can do nothing, but together can decide nothing can be done.

—*Fred Allen (1894–1956)*

# Complaints

What we all tend to complain about most in other people are those things we don't like in ourselves.
—*William Wharton,* Tidings *(Henry Holt & Co.)*

A customer who complains is doing you a great service.

# Communication—Verbal

Two monologues do not make a dialogue.

There is nothing so annoying as arguing with a man who knows what he is talking about.

You can be an expert in your subject but not an expert in communicating that subject.

You cannot antagonize and persuade at the same time.

The most important thing in communication is to hear what isn't being said.

A gossip is one who talks to you about others; a bore is one who talks to you about himself; a brilliant conversationalist is one who talks to you about yourself.

I don't know if you know this, but a recent scientific study has shown that the average man speaks 25,000 words a day, and the average woman, 30,000. Unfortunately, when I come home each day, I've already spoken my 25,000—and my wife hasn't started her 30,000. Therefore, since I have already used up a week's worth of my words today with you, and, lest I be forced to listen to my wife uninterrupted for the next month, I think I had better come to an end of this talk.

Studies have shown that humans can hear and comprehend up to 600 words per minute, but most people speak around 120 words per minute. Therefore, the human mind wanders to fill in the gaps. The Stanford University Social Studies Center surveyed 10,000 people on what else they were thinking about during a controlled talking/listening experiment. About two-thirds of the people (almost 7,000) were thinking of sex. Therefore, two-thirds of this audience will be smiling and having a good time no matter what I say or do here today.

It usually takes me more than three weeks to prepare a good impromptu speech. —*Mark Twain (1835–1910)*

Words are the most powerful drug used by mankind.
—*Rudyard Kipling (1865–1936)*

Sam Goldwyn, famous movie producer, was also famous for his colorful, if not confusing, style of speaking. A few of Sam's more memorable lines include:
A verbal contract isn't worth the paper it's printed on.
Every Tom, Dick, and Harry is named William.
Now, gentlemen, listen slowly.
For your information, I would like to ask a question.
Include me out.
Don't talk to me when I'm interrupting.
I may not always be right, but I'm never wrong.

Wise men talk because they have something to say; fools, because they have to say something.
—*Plato (ca. 427–347 B.C.)*

The importance of tact in communications is demonstrated by Helen and her brother, Bob. When Helen went out of town on vacation, she asked Bob to come by each day and take care of her prized cat. She called from her hotel the next night and asked how the cat was, to which Bob curtly responded, "Oh, your cat's dead."

Helen was aghast at the news and shouted, "Bob, how could you be so insensitive! You know how I loved that cat! At least, you could have broken the news to me gradually. One day, you could say that the cat was stuck on the roof. The next day, you could say that the fire department came and tried to rescue the cat, but it jumped from the roof and injured itself. Then, on the third day, after I was prepared, you could have told me that

the vet did everything possible, but the cat passed away." After regaining her composure from the news and having criticized Bob adequately, she asked, "Well, how's Mother?"

There was silence for a moment until Bob replied in a soft voice, "She's on the roof."

Communication doesn't flow. Sometimes it leaks, spurts, and dribbles.

George Bernard Shaw was once complimented on his public-speaking abilities and was asked how he developed them. He responded, "I learned to speak as men learn to skate or cycle, by doggedly making a fool of myself until I got used to it."

## Communication—Written

General Billy Mitchell, father of the U.S. Air Force, found that when his orders were not followed, it was because they were not understood. "I always kept an officer at my headquarters to whom I could read all orders," he said. "If he could understand them, anybody could. He was not particularly bright, but he was one of my most useful officers for that reason."

No passion in the world, no love or hate, is equal to the passion to alter someone else's draft.     —*H. G. Wells (1866–1946)*

Words are things, and a small drop of ink, falling like dew upon a thought, produces that which makes thousands, perhaps millions, think.     —*Walt Whitman (1819–1892)*

Every communication a manager makes does two things: It conveys ideas and it generates feelings. The reader's feelings, needs and motives must be considered as well as his literacy level.

Writing letters of recommendation can be hazardous; tell the truth and you might get sued if the contents are negative. Robert Thornton, a professor at Lehigh University, has a collection of "virtually litigation-proof" phrases called the Lexicon of Intentionally Ambiguous Recommendations, or LIAR. Here are some examples:

   To describe an inept person: "I enthusiastically recommend this candidate with no qualifications whatsoever."

   To describe an ex-employee who had problems getting along with co-workers: "I am pleased to say that this candidate is a former colleague of mine."

   To describe an unproductive candidate: "I can assure you that no person would be better for the job."

   To describe an applicant not worth considering: "I would urge you to waste no time in making this candidate an offer of employment."

                     —*Larry Prior in* Los Angeles Times

A messenger delivered a telegram to a young man from his fiancée: "COME DOWN AS SOON AS YOU CAN; I AM DYING. KATE." Obviously shocked, the young man struggled for eight hours of travel until he arrived at his fiancée's home, only to find her sitting on the front porch. "Why did you send me such a shocking message. . . . You appear to be fine!" queried the young man.

"Oh, dear," she said, "I wanted to say that I was dying to see you, but my ten words ran out and I had to stop."

Possible communication errors taken from actual church bulletins:

This being Easter Sunday, we will ask Mrs. Jackson to come forward and lay an egg on the altar.

The ladies of the church have cast-off clothing of every kind. They may be seen in the basement of the church on Friday afternoon.

Tuesday at 4 p.m. there will be an ice cream social. Will ladies giving milk, please come early.

Thursday at 5 p.m. is a meeting of the Little Mothers Club. All wishing to become Little Mothers should meet the pastor in his study.

Examples of unclear writing taken from letters received by a Welfare Department requesting support:

I am pleased to report that my husband, who was missing, is dead.

I have given birth to a son weighing ten pounds. I hope this is satisfactory.

I am much annoyed that you have branded my son illiterate. This is a dirty lie, as I was married a full week before he was born.

I've been in bed with the doctor for two weeks now. He doesn't do any good. If things don't improve, I'll have to send for another doctor.

My husband had his project cut off two months ago and I haven't had any relief since.

As you can see, I have given birth to twins in the enclosed envelope.

Examples of unclear writing taken from newspaper stories:

AB, who joined the Bank of Commerce more than a year ago as an installment loan officer and made advances to the supervisor of the Installment Loan Department, was named an assistant vice-president.

Bring your newspapers (and your neighbors). Put them in paper bags or tie them if possible.

LOST: Male cat. Needs medication. Owner very worried, neutered and declawed.

After tea, Mrs. X gave an amusing talk, with slides, on Baboo, her pet baboon. She said that although some people were scared by such a large animal, she felt completely at home with him, having spent 15 years in Africa with her husband.

# Complexities

There is no subject, however simple or complex, which—if studied with patience and intelligence—will not become more complex.

The easier it is to do, the harder is it to change.

Out of intense complexities intense simplicities emerge.
—*Winston Churchill (1874–1965)*

# Conscience

He that hath a blind conscience which sees nothing, a dead conscience which feels nothing, and a dumb conscience which says nothing, is in as miserable condition as a man can be on this side of hell.   —*Patrick Henry (1736–1799)*

Conscience: Something that feels terrible when everything else feels swell.

A guilty conscience is the mother of invention.

In matters of conscience, the law of majority has no place.
—*Mohandas K. Gandhi (1869–1948)*

As long as your conscience is your friend, never mind about your enemies.

Conscience warns you as a friend before it punishes you as a judge.

Conscience: An inner voice that warns us that somebody is looking. —*H. L. Mencken (1880–1956)*

Conscience is what makes you tell your wife something before someone else does.

## Consistency

Consistency is the last refuge of the unimaginative.
—*Oscar Wilde (1854–1900)*

The only completely consistent people are the dead.
—*Aldous Huxley (1894–1963)*, Essays

## Cooperation

Coming together is a beginning; keeping together is progress; working together is success. —*Henry Ford (1863–1947)*

## Courage

Some have been thought brave because they were afraid to run away. —*Thomas Fuller (1608–1661)*

Courage is not freedom from fear; it is being afraid and going on.

It is not enough to have the courage to do the right thing—it must also be done in the right way.

Keep your fears to yourself; share your courage with others.
—*Robert Louis Stevenson (1850–1894)*

Courage is resistance to fear, mastery of fear—not absence of fear. —*Mark Twain (1835–1910)*

It takes as much courage to try and fail as it does to try and succeed.

## Data/Computers/Technology

Technology is dominated by those who manage what they do not understand.

New systems generate new problems.

Any sufficiently advanced technology is indistinguishable from magic.

What are the best and worst aspects of computers that will be doing our thinking for us someday? They have no emotions, and they have no emotions.

Computers are unreliable, but humans are even more unreliable; any system which depends on human reliability is unreliable.

Under the most rigorously controlled conditions of pressure, temperature, volume, humidity, and other variables, the organism will do as it damn well pleases.

If it's not in the computer, it doesn't exist.

First Law of Systems Planning: Anything that can be changed will be changed until there is no time left to change anything.

Technology is the most subtle and the most effective engineer of enduring social change. Its apparent neutrality is deceptive and often disarming. —*Robert MacIver*

# Death

It's not that I'm afraid to die, I just don't want to be there when it happens. —*Woody Allen (1935– )*

It's a funny old world—a man's lucky if he can get out of it alive. —*W. C. Fields (1880–1946)*

If you don't go to people's funerals, they won't come to yours.

When a man is still living, we estimate his power and value by his worst performance or characteristics; once he is dead, we remember and measure him only by his best.

Why is it that we rejoice at a birth and grieve at a funeral? Is it because we are not the person involved?
—*Mark Twain (1835–1910)*

32

Grief knits two hearts in closer bonds than happiness ever can; and common sufferings are far stronger links than common joys.     —*Alphonse-Marie-Louis de Lamartine (1790–1869)*

Why do flags fly at half-mast when someone dies? After a naval battle, it used to be custom for the defeated ship to lower its flag to signal surrender and make room for the victor's flag above it. Apparently, after this tradition faded, a lowered flag continued to be used as a universal sign of respect.
—*Douglas B. Smith*, Ever Wonder Why? *(Ballantine Books)*

It is the cause, and not the death, that makes the martyr.
                    —*Napoleon Bonaparte (1769–1821)*

Mike was about to die and the priest bent over him to give him the last rites of the Church. Bending over Mike, the priest said, "Repeat after me, 'I renounce the devil and all his evil deeds.' "

But there was no response from Mike. The priest repeated, "Repeat after me, 'I renounce the devil and all his evil deeds,' " and still no response from Mike. After the third try, the priest shook Mike and he opened his eyes. "Didn't you hear me?" asked the priest.

"Yes," replied Mike, "But you told me I was going to die, and this is a hell of a time to antagonize anybody."

—*Jacob Braude*, Speaker's Encyclopedia *(Prentice-Hall)*

Any man who has $10,000 left when he dies is a failure.

—*Errol Flynn (1909–1959)*

## Decisions/Decision-Making

The fine art of executive decision consists in not deciding questions that are not now pertinent, in not deciding prematurely, in not making decisions that cannot be made effective, and in not making decisions that others should make.

—*Chester I. Barnard (1886–1961)*

Standing in the middle of the road is very dangerous; you get knocked down by the traffic from both sides.

—*Margaret Thatcher (1925–    )*

Even if you're on the right track, you'll get run over if you just sit there.

Decisiveness is not in itself a virtue. To decide not to decide is a decision; to fail to decide is a failure.

Nothing will ever be attempted if all possible objections must first be overcome.

When you have to make a choice and don't make it, that is in itself a choice.

It does not take much strength to do things, but it requires great strength to decide on what to do.

If everyone is thinking alike then somebody isn't thinking.

—*General George Patton (1885–1945)*

34

The best time to make a decision is before you have to make one.

A person always has two reasons for doing anything—a good reason and the real reason.

—*J. Pierpont Morgan (1837–1913)*

## Details

Don't be more precise than the subject warrants.

—*Plato (ca. 427–347 B.C.)*

We think in generalities, but we live in detail.

—*Alfred North Whitehead (1861–1947)*

Beware of the man who won't be bothered with details.

35

The hottest places in hell are reserved for those who, in times of great moral crisis, maintain their neutrality.

—*Dante (1265–1321)*

A decision is what a man reluctantly makes when he can't get anyone to form a committee.

Lord, when we are wrong, make us willing to change. And when we are right, make us easy to live with.

## Diet

The doctor decided to put his overweight patient on a diet. "I want you to eat regularly for two days," the physician directed, "then skip a day, and repeat this procedure for two weeks. The next time I see you, you should have lost at least five pounds."

When the man returned, he had lost twenty pounds. "You did this just by following my instructions?" the doctor asked.

The fellow nodded. "I'll tell you, though, I thought I was going to drop dead that third day."

"From hunger?"

"No, from skipping."

—*Jeff Rovin*, 1,001 Great Jokes *(Signet)*

We never repent of having eaten too little.

—*Thomas Jefferson (1743–1826)*

The inequality of the world can be seen in the fact that two-thirds are starving and one-third are dieting.

I have been on a constant diet for the last two decades. I've lost a total of 789 pounds. By all accounts, I should be hanging from a charm bracelet. —*Erma Bombeck*

He was a very valiant man who first adventured on eating oysters. —*Thomas Fuller (1608–1661)*

They have digged their graves with their teeth.

—*Thomas Adams (1612–1653)*

The Rule of the Rabbi: If you're really dying to eat it, don't ask if it's kosher.

Doctor to overweight patient: "And this medication should be taken on an empty stomach, Mr. Jones—if such an opportunity ever presents itself.

I went on a diet, swore off drinking and heavy eating, and in fourteen days I had lost exactly two weeks.

—*Joe E. Lewis (1902–1971)*

## Diplomacy

A true diplomat is someone who can tell you to go to hell in a way that makes you look forward to the trip.

You can't carve out a good career with cutting remarks.

Tact is the ability to describe others as they see themselves.
—*Abraham Lincoln (1809–1865)*

# Ecology

If you don't care about slum children while you are worrying about bald eagles, well, you are just getting your priorities a bit wrong. —*Barbara Ward (1914–1981)*

There were about 8,000 cars in the United States, only ten miles of concrete pavement, and few spray cans to destroy the ozone layer. Everyone ate natural foods. The air was relatively unpolluted, and the ground was free of aluminum cans. There were no sugar substitutes and no artificial coloring. We had no atomic waste or PCBs, and our average life expectancy was 47 years. The year was 1900. Today we are doing everything wrong, and the life expectancy is up to 75 years, and if we are not careful, it could hit 90.

—*William J. McIlrath, quoted in* Reader's Digest, *November 1989. Reprinted with permission from the November 1989* Reader's Digest. *Copyright © 1989 by the Reader's Digest Assn., Inc.*

I shot an arrow into the air . . . and it stuck.
—*Graffiti in Los Angeles*

# Economics

Blessed are the young, for they shall inherit the national debt.
—*Herbert Hoover (1874–1964)*

It's recession when your neighbor loses his job; it's a depression when you lose your own.
—*Harry S Truman (1884–1972)*

Why is it that it seems the poor have more children, but the rich have more relatives?

Christmas is a time when children ask Santa Claus for what they want and adults pay for it. Deficits are when adults spend what they want and children pay for it.

—*Richard Lamm, former Governor of Colorado*

## Education

The only thing more expensive than education is ignorance.
—*Benjamin Franklin (1706–1790)*

I am always ready to learn, although I do not always like being taught. —*Winston Churchill (1874–1965)*

I have never let my schooling interfere with my education.
—*Mark Twain (1835–1910)*

Academic and aristocratic people live in such an uncommon atmosphere that common sense can rarely reach them.

*—Samuel Butler (1835–1902)*

Old Principals never die . . . they just lose their faculties.


Principals are not necessarily smarter than other people, they just have their ignorance better organized.

To educate a man in mind and not in morals is to educate a menace to society.          *—Theodore Roosevelt (1858–1919)*

Public schools are the nurseries of all vice and immorality.

*—Henry Fielding (1707–1754)*

In the first place God made idiots. This was for practice. Then He made School Boards.          *—Mark Twain (1835–1910)*

The schools ain't what they used to be and never was.

—*Will Rogers (1879–1935)*

A parent who sends his son into the world uneducated and without skill in any art or science does a great injury to mankind as well as to his own family, for he defrauds the community of a useful citizen and bequeaths to it a nuisance.

—*James Kent (1763—1847)*

What sculpture is to a block of marble, education is to a human soul.
—*Joseph Addison (1672–1719)*

The teacher decided to ask her students some math questions. "Johnny, if candy is selling at $2 a pound and you pay the storekeeper $8, how many pounds will he bring you?"

Johnny quickly responded, "A little over 3 pounds, ma'am."

"Well, Johnny, that isn't right," replied the teacher.

"No, ma'am, I know it ain't," said Johnny, "but they all do it."

A child educated only at school is an uneducated child.

—*George Santayana (1863–1952)*

A man who has never gone to school may steal from a freight car; but if he has a university education, he may steal the whole railroad.
—*Theodore Roosevelt (1858–1919)*

The education of a man is never completed until he dies.

—*Robert E. Lee (1807–1870)*

Education is not the filling of a pail, but the lighting of a fire.
—*William Butler Yeats (1865–1939)*

# Effort

Edward's Time/Effort Law: Effort $\times$ Time = Constant.

Efforts and courage are not enough without purpose and direction.
—*John F. Kennedy (1917–1963)*

It is not the load that breaks you down; it is the way you carry it.

Either do not attempt at all, or go through with it.

—*Ovid (ca. 43 B.C.–A.D. 17)*

It's easier to agree to do better tomorrow than to do your best today.

Stanley Baldwin, former prime minister of England, quoted these lines in the House of Commons: "The halls of fame are open wide and they are always full. Some go in by the door called 'push,' and some by the door called 'pull.' "

The only place where success comes before work is in the dictionary.

To do two things at once is to do neither.

—*Publilius Syrus (fl. 1st century B.C.)*

It is one thing to itch for something and another to scratch for it.

The harder you work, the harder it is to surrender.

—*Vince Lombardi (1913–1970)*

Of those to whom much is given, much is required.

—*John F. Kennedy (1917–1963)*

Doing your best is more important than being the best.

Don't measure yourself by what you have accomplished, but by what you should have accomplished with your ability.

—*Former UCLA Basketball Coach John Wooden*

If I were to read, much less answer, all the attacks made on me, this shop might as well be closed for any other business. I do the very best I know how—the very best I can; and I mean to keep doing so until the end. If the end brings me out all right, what is said against me won't amount to anything. If the end brings me out wrong, ten thousand angels swearing I was right would make no difference.   —*Abraham Lincoln (1809–1865)*

The man who moves a mountain begins by carrying away small stones. —*Confucius (551–479 B.C.)*

It's not whether you get knocked down, it's whether you get up. —*Vince Lombardi (1913–1970)*

Everything comes to him who hustles while he waits.
—*Thomas Edison (1847–1931)*

## Employment/Hiring

A Princeton graduate applied for a job at a major department store in Philadelphia. The personnel manager wrote to one of the fellow's references and received a lengthy reply, detailing the applicant's fine social standing and family background, from Pilgrim stock. "Sir," the personnel manager responded, "I

43

think you misunderstood. We want to employ the young man for business purposes, not breeding purposes."

—*Thomas Kean, former New Jersey Governor*

A confident applicant for a job presented his credentials to a personnel manager. The manager looked them over and said, "I see you've got recommendations from your church minister and Sunday-school teacher. That's good. And, I must admit, you look honest and appear to be of good character. Nevertheless, I'd like to see a recommendation from someone who knows you on weekdays."

Every organization has an allotted number of positions to be filled by misfits.

A businessman of rather shabby reputation was interviewing applicants for the job of chief accountant. He asked each, "How much is two plus two?"

The first two applicants replied, "Four." Neither got the job. The third was hired.

When asked the sum of two plus two, he got up, closed the door, drew the blinds, leaned across the desk and said, "How much would you like it to be?"

An employer interviewing an applicant remarked, "You ask high wages for a man with no experience."

"Well," the prospect replied, "It's so much harder to work when you don't know anything about it."

A manager called an employee into his office. "I know you're aware of our need for budget cuts, so I'll get straight to the point. I've got some good news and some bad news. The good news is I've decided to double your salary. The bad news is I have to fire you . . . but I'll be saving twice as much money."

# Examinations

Examinations are formidable even to the best prepared; for the greatest fool may ask more than the wisest man can answer.
—*Charles Colton (1780–1832)*

If you are given an open-book exam, you will forget your book. If you are given a take-home exam, you will forget where you live.

If mathematically you come up with the wrong answer, try multiplying by the page number.

A student had failed to appear at school on the day of an important test, so I attempted to call his home. Unsuccessful, I walked back to class only to see the tardy pupil come panting up the stairs. He was ashen. "Did you know," he asked in a tone of agony, "that Scope mouthwash and Prell shampoo are both green?"

# Experience

If we could sell our experiences for what they cost us, we'd all be millionaires.

A man had expected to be promoted upon the retirement of his boss. When the job was given to a more capable younger man, he protested. "But I've had twenty years' experience!"

"No," he was told, "In reality, you've haven't had twenty years' experience. You've had one year's experience twenty times over."


Mark Twain was leaving church one day with his friend William Dean Howells when it started to rain heavily. Howells glanced at the deluge and said, "Do you think it will stop?"

"It always has," replied Twain.


Experience is the name everyone gives to their mistakes.
—*Oscar Wilde (1854–1900)*

I have but one lamp by which my feet are guided, and that is the lamp of experience. I know of no way of judging the future but by the past.        —*Patrick Henry (1736–1799)*

Experience teaches us that experience teaches nothing.

If only one could have two lives: the first in which to make one's mistakes, and the second in which to profit by them.

Experience is not what happens to a man. It is what a man does with what happens to him.     —*Aldous Huxley (1894–1963)*

A small factory had to stop operations when an essential piece of machinery broke down. No one could get the machine operating, so an outside expert was finally called in. The fellow looked over the situation for a moment, then took a hammer and gently tapped the machine at a certain spot. It began running again immediately and continued to run as if nothing had ever been wrong. When the expert submitted his bill for $100, the plant supervisor hit the ceiling and demanded an itemized

bill. The bill the man submitted was as follows: For hitting machine, $1. For knowing where to hit, $99.

You need a track record before people are willing to bet on you.

A little experience upsets a lot of theory.
—*S. Parkes Cadman (1864–1936)*

We should be careful to get out of an experience only the wisdom that is in it—and stop there, lest we be like the cat that sits down on the hot stove-lid. She will never sit down on a hot stove-lid again, and that is well; but she also will never sit down on a cold one.　　　　—*Mark Twain (1835–1910)*

Experience does not err; it is only your judgment that errs in expecting from her what is not in her power.
—*Leonardo da Vinci (1452–1519)*

Good judgment comes from experience, and experience comes from bad judgment.

Experience is the comb that Nature gives us when we are bald.
—*Belgian proverb*

Experience enables you to recognize a mistake right after you made it again.

It is a good thing to learn caution by the misfortune of others.
—*Publilius Syrus* (fl. *1st century* B.C.)

## Experts

You can't always go by expert opinion. A turkey, if you ask a turkey, should be stuffed with grasshoppers, grit, and worms.
—Changing Times, *The Kiplinger Magazine*

An expert is one who knows more and more about less and less until he knows absolutely everything about nothing.

To spot the expert, pick the one who says the job will take the longest and cost the most.


Expert: A person who can take something you already know and make it sound confusing.

The expert in anything was once a beginner.


Be careful about calling yourself an "expert." An "ex" is a has-been, and a "spurt" is a drip under pressure.

## Facts

There are no facts, only interpretations.
                                   —*Friedrich Nietzsche (1844–1900)*

Facts do not cease to exist because they are ignored.
                                   —*Aldous Huxley (1894–1963)*

Get your facts first, and then you can distort them as much as you please.          —*Mark Twain (1835–1910)*

I'm always fascinated by the memory that diffuses fact.


## Failure

All too many of us have as our objective not to be successful, but rather to see how long we can postpone failure.

If at first you don't succeed, try, try again. Then quit. No use being a damn fool about it.     —*W. C. Fields (1880–1946)*

A word of encouragement during a failure is worth more than a whole book of praise after a success.

We have forty million reasons for failure, but not a single excuse. —*Rudyard Kipling (1865–1936)*

The taste of defeat has a richness of experience all its own.

If at first you don't succeed, destroy all evidence that you ever tried.

Failure is the greatest opportunity I have to know who I really am. —*John Killinger, Representative from Pennsylvania (1825–1896)*

The only difference between stumbling blocks and stepping stones is how you use them.

Every man's got to figure to get beat sometimes. —*Joe Louis (1914–    )*

Failure is only the opportunity to begin again more intelligently. —*Henry Ford (1863–1947)*

In great attempts it is glorious even to fail. —*Vince Lombardi (1913–1970)*

It's a lonesome walk to the sidelines, especially when thousands of people are cheering your replacement. —*Fran Tarkenton, former Minnesota Vikings quarterback*

Our greatest glory is not in never failing, but in rising every time we fail. —*Confucius (551–479 B.C.)*

Disappointment to a noble soul is what cold water means to burning metal; it strengthens, tempers, intensifies, but never destroys it. —*Eliza Tabor (1835–1914)*

It is hard to fail, but it is worse never to have tried to succeed. —*Theodore Roosevelt (1858–1919)*

No one knows what to say in the loser's room. —*Muhammad Ali (1942–    )*

People may fail many times, but they become failures only when they begin to blame someone else.

Everyone's allowed an occasional failure—except the skydiver, of course.

Success is never final, failure never fatal.

## Faith

Sorrow looks back, worry looks around, faith looks up.

God hides things by putting them near us.
—*Ralph Waldo Emerson (1803–1882)*

All that I have seen teaches me to trust the Creator for all I have not seen. —*Ralph Waldo Emerson (1803–1882)*

All the darkness in the world can't put out the light of one candle. —*Confucius (551–479 B.C.)*

We couldn't conceive of a miracle if none had ever happened.

Faith keeps the person that keeps the faith.

I am like a little pencil in God's hand. He does the writing. The pencil has nothing to do with it.

—*Mother Teresa (1910–     )*

What good is it for someone to say that he has faith if his actions do not prove it?                    —*James 2:14*

Faith is illuminative, not operative; it does not force obedience, though it increases responsibility; it heightens guilt, but it does not prevent sin.          —*Cardinal Newman (1801–1890)*

Faith is never identical to piety.    —*Karl Barth (1886–1968)*

Whatever is the subject of faith should not be submitted to reason, and much less should bend to it.

—*Blaise Pascal (1623–1662)*

In a sensational court case, the plaintiff, who was all twisted and bent over, won $3 million from the driver of another car. The defendant was sure the "injured party" was faking, so after the trial he followed the guy around everywhere, even trailing him to France. "Where do we go now?" the defendant taunted the plaintiff.

"Off to Lourdes! If you watch closely, you'll see one of the greatest miracles of all time."

—*Alex Thien in Milwaukee* Sentinel

A rather famous entertainer was traveling back from a two-week goodwill trip to China. On the same boat was a missionary who had worked with the poor in China for many years. When they docked in New York, the missionary saw a crowd of the entertainer's fans waiting at the pier. "Lord, I don't understand," the missionary said. "I gave 42 years of my life to China, and he gave only two weeks, yet there are thousands welcoming him home and nobody here to welcome me."

And the Lord replied, "Son, you're not home yet."
—*William Cross and Michael Kosser*, The Conway Twitty
Story *(Doubleday)*

Some things have to be believed to be seen.
—*Ralph Hodgson*, The Skylark and Other Poems
*(Macmillan, London)*

## Family

The purpose of my evening walk is the walking itself, and the mental, emotional, and physical benefits it brings. But the ultimate goal is a different perspective. As I return from my contemplative constitutional, there on the corner stands my house. From across the street I pause and look. I think of our three young sons asleep upstairs, and of my wife who sits in the living room reading, or in the study as she plays her guitar and sings quietly to herself. I take a deep breath of the clean night air and think, "In that house is all that is most precious to me." That is the main reason that I walk one mile away from home each evening, then one mile back, and then pause: to remind myself of the sacred things in my life.
—*Mitch Finley in* The Christian Science Monitor

Blood is thicker than water, and it boils quicker.

Fond as we are of our loved ones, there comes at times during their absence an unexplainable peace.
—*Ann Shaw*, But Such Is Life *(Cecil Palmer, England)*

He that has no fools, knaves nor beggars in his *family* was begot by a flash of lightning.   —*Thomas Fuller (1608–1661)*

## Faults

Always acknowledge a fault frankly. This will throw those in charge off guard and give you the opportunity to commit more.
—*Mark Twain (1835–1910)*

The greatest of faults is to be conscious of none.
—*Thomas Carlyle (1795–1881)*

Don't tell your friends their faults. They will correct the fault and never forgive you.

## Fools

Let us be thankful for the fools. But for them, the rest of us could not succeed. —*Mark Twain (1835–1910)*

Don't ever forget that you are part of the people who can be fooled some of the time.

If fifty million people say a foolish thing, it is still a foolish thing. —*Anatole France (1844–1924)*

Fools make feasts, and wise men eat them.

—*Benjamin Franklin (1706–1790)*

The greatest lesson in life is to know that even fools are right sometimes. —*Winston Churchill (1874–1965)*

Any fool can criticize, condemn and complain, and most do.
—*Dale Carnegie,* How to Win Friends and Influence People
*(Pocket Books)*

# Friends/Friendship

A friend is someone who knows all about you but likes you anyway.

Am I not destroying my enemies when I make friends of them?
—*Abraham Lincoln (1809–1865)*

A real friend is a person who, when you've made a fool of yourself, lets you forget it.

My best friend is the one who brings out the best in me.
—*Henry Ford (1863–1947)*

It takes your enemy and your friend, working together, to hurt you to the heart; the one to slander you and the other to get the news to you. —*Mark Twain (1835–1910)*

A true friend is someone who is there for you when he'd rather be anywhere else.

In life it is difficult to say who does you the most mischief— enemies with the worst intentions or friends with the best.
—*Sir Henry Bulwer (1801–1872)*

You can make more friends in two months by becoming interested in other people than you can in two years by trying to get people interested in you. —*Dale Carnegie*

Winning has always meant much to me, but winning friends has meant the most.—*Babe Didrikson Zaharias (1914—1956)*

A friend may well be reckoned the masterpiece of Nature.
—*Ralph Waldo Emerson (1803–1882)*

The meeting of two personalities is like the contact of two chemical substances: if there is any reaction, both are transformed. —*C. G. Jung (1875–1961)*

False friends are like our shadows, keeping close to us while we walk in the sunshine, but leaving us the instant we cross into the shade. —*Christian Nestell Bovee*

## Future

My interest is in the future, because I am going to spend the rest of my life there. —*Charles Kettering (1876–1958)*

I never think of the future. It comes soon enough.
—*Albert Einstein (1879–1955)*

The best thing about the future is that it comes only one day at a time. —*Abraham Lincoln (1809–1865)*

There has never been an age that did not applaud the past and lament the future.
—*Lillian Eichler Watson*, Light From Many Lamps *(Simon & Schuster)*

The past is but the beginning of a beginning, and all that is and has been is but the twilight of the dawn.
—*H. G. Wells (1866–1946)*

I like the dreams of the future better than the history of the past. —*Thomas Jefferson (1743–1826)*

# General

No bird soars too high, if it soars with its own wings.
—*William Blake (1757–1827)*

Logic is a systematic way of coming to the wrong conclusion with confidence.

All's well that ends.

What seems so necessary today may not even be desirable tomorrow.

Nobody goes to that restaurant anymore. It's too crowded.
—*Yogi Berra (1925–     )*

Such is the human race. Often it does seem such a pity that Noah and his party didn't miss the boat.
—*Mark Twain (1835–1910)*

One of the most serious thoughts that life provokes is the reflection that we can never tell, at the time, whether a word, a look, a touch, an occurrence of any kind, is trivial or important.

"Maintenance-free" usually means that when it breaks, it can't be fixed.

A diplomat is a man who makes you feel at home—even if he wishes you were.

The thing to do is supply light and not heat.

—*Woodrow Wilson (1856–1924)*

Now this is not the end. It is not even the beginning of the end. But it is, perhaps, the end of the beginning.

—*Winston Churchill (1874–1965)*

## Giving

If you give what you do not need, it isn't giving.

—*Mother Teresa (1910–      )*

Give what you have. To someone, it may be better than you dare think.     —*Henry Wadsworth Longfellow (1784–1864)*

# God

We trust sir, that God is on our side. It is more important to know that we are on God's side.

                          —*Abraham Lincoln (1809–1865)*

God does not pay by the week, but he pays at the end.

                                          —*Dutch proverb*

What you are is God's gift to you; what you make of yourself is your gift to God.

The knowledge of God is very far from the love of Him.

                                —*Blaise Pascal (1623–1662)*

If God lived on earth, people would break His windows.

                                        —*Yiddish proverb*

God is the Supreme Comic, but He plays to an audience who refuses to laugh.

      —*Rev. Paul Mueller, Vicar of Priests, Diocese of Toledo*

Grace is God taking you out for a milkshake after a baseball game whether you go 3 for 4 or 0 for 5.

If you are not guided by God, you will be guided by someone or something else.

# Gossip

Some people will believe anything if it is whispered to them.

There are many who dare not kill themselves for fear of what the neighbors would say.     —*Cyril Connolly (1903–1974)*

There would not be so many open mouths if there were not so many open ears.     —*Bishop Hall (1574–1656)*

There are two good rules which ought to be written on every heart. Never believe anything bad about anybody, unless you positively know that it is true. Never tell even that, unless you feel that it is absolutely necessary, and that God is listening while you tell it.

Four ministers were walking in the park one day before an ecumenical meeting, chatting about the trials and tribulations

of being men of the cloth. One of their common problems, they decided, was their inability to have close friends with whom they could share their most personal problems. They decided to confide in one another. The first began by confiding to the others that he had a significant drinking problem. The others showed surprise at this revelation, but it inspired them to also share their innermost secrets. The second clergyman then spoke up, informing his cohorts that he was growing increasingly fond of a married woman in his congregation. The third confided that he had, on occasion, dipped into the collection plate to help support his gambling habit. The fourth minister said nothing. Finally, after urging from the three who had confessed their darkest secrets, he could resist their pressure no longer. "I know my secret vice will be more shocking and disturbing to you than any you have heard so far." The others coaxed him on, assuring him that his secret would be safe with them. "Okay then, here it is—you see, I am an incurable gossip."

In our appetite for gossip, we tend to gobble down everything before us, only to find, too late, that it is our ideals that we have consumed, and we have not been enlarged by the feasts but only diminished.                                        —*Pico Iyer in* Time

## Government

Be thankful we're not getting all the government we're paying for.                                        —*Will Rogers (1879–1935)*

The illegal we do immediately. The unconstitutional takes a little longer.                                        —*Henry Kissinger (1923–     )*

Too bad all the people who know how to run the country are busy driving taxicabs and cutting hair.

—*George Burns (1896–     )*

It is by the goodness of God that we have in our country three unspeakably precious things: freedom of speech, freedom of conscience, and the prudence never to practice either.

—*Mark Twain (1835–1910)*

The impersonal hand of government can never replace the helping hand of a neighbor. —*Hubert H. Humphrey (1911–1978)*

The government is best which governs least.

—*Thomas Jefferson (1743–1826)*

61

# Habits

Nothing so needs reforming as other people's habits.
*—Mark Twain (1835–1910)*

The chains of habit are generally too small to be felt until they are too strong to be broken. *—Samuel Johnson (1709–1784)*

It is easier to suppress the first desire than to satisfy all that follow it. *—Benjamin Franklin (1706–1790)*

Form good habits. They're as hard to break as bad ones.

Excellence is not an act but a habit.

*—Aristotle (384–322 B.C.)*

# Happiness

Some cause happiness wherever they go; others whenever they go.  —*Oscar Wilde (1854–1900)*

If ignorance is bliss, why aren't more people happy?

You cannot pour happiness on others without getting a few drops on yourself.  —*Ralph Waldo Emerson (1803–1882)*

Happiness is a conscious choice, not an automatic response.

Happiness, in this world, if it comes at all, comes incidentally. Make it the object of pursuit, and it leads us on a wild-goose chase, and it is never attained.

—*Nathaniel Hawthorne (1804–1864)*

Happiness comes from feeling deeply, enjoying simply, and thinking freely.

People are never as happy or unhappy as they think.

Happiness lies in the joy of achievement and the thrill of creative effort.　　　　　—*Franklin D. Roosevelt (1882–1945)*

We have no more right to consume happiness without producing it than to consume wealth without producing it.
　　　　　—*George Bernard Shaw (1856–1950)*

Happiness makes up in height for what it lacks in length.
　　　　　—*Robert Frost (1874–1963)*

It's pretty hard to tell what does bring happiness; poverty and wealth have both failed.　　　　　—*Kin Hubbard (1868–1930)*

When I was young, I used to think that wealth and power would bring me happiness. I was right.　　　—*Gahan Wilson*

Happiness is good health and a bad memory.
　　　　　—*Ingrid Bergman (1915–1982)*


# History

History is more or less bunk.　　　　　—*Henry Ford (1863–1947)*

All the ancient histories are but fables that have been agreed upon.　　　　　—*Voltaire (1694–1778)*

Those who cannot remember the past are condemned to repeat it.　　　　　—*George Santayana (1863–1952)*

History is the science of what never happens twice.
　　　　　—*Paul Valéry (1871–1945)*

Charles A. Beard, the historian, was asked what lessons he had learned from all the history he knew. His reply was:
1. When it gets darkest, the stars come out.
2. When a bee steals from a flower, it also fertilizes it.

3. Whom the gods would destroy, they first make mad with power.
4. Though the mills of God grind slowly, yet they grind exceedingly small.       —*Jacob Braude (1955–     )*

History teaches us that men and nations behave wisely once they have exhausted all other alternatives.
       —*Abba Eban (1915–     )*

The trouble with each new generation is that they don't take the time to read the minutes of the last meeting.

History was a trash bag of random coincidences torn open by the wind. Surely, Watt with his steam engine, Faraday with his electric motor, and Edison with his incandescent light bulb did not have it as their goal to contribute to a fuel shortage some day that would place their countries at the mercy of Arab oil.
       —*Joseph Heller,* Catch-22

It has been said that though God cannot alter the past, historians can; it is perhaps because they can be useful to Him in this respect that He tolerates their existence.
       —*Samuel Butler (1835–1902)*

What we learn from the past is that we seldom learn from the past.


# Honesty

It's discouraging to think how many people are shocked by honesty and how few by deceit.       —*Noël Coward,* Blithe Spirit

A truly honest man creates the same impression on everyone.

It is easier to be honest with others than with ourselves.

# Honors

No person was ever honored for what he received. Honor has been the reward for what he gave.

—*Calvin Coolidge (1872–1933)*

It is better to deserve honors and not have them than to have them and not deserve them.     —*Mark Twain (1835–1910)*

The people most preoccupied with honors, titles, and status are usually the least deserving of them.

# Human Characteristics

There are two tragedies in life. One is to lose your heart's desire. The other is to gain it.

—*George Bernard Shaw (1856–1950)*

What you do speaks so loudly that I cannot hear what you say.

Always do right. This will gratify some people, and astonish the rest.     —*Mark Twain (1835–1910)*

He reminds me of the man who murdered both his parents, and then, when his sentence was about to be pronounced, pleaded for mercy on the grounds that he was an orphan.

—*Abraham Lincoln (1809–1865)*

If a man could have half his wishes, he would double his troubles.     —*Benjamin Franklin (1706–1790)*

I believe that our Heavenly Father invented man only because He was disappointed in the monkey.

—*Mark Twain (1835–1910)*

People have a way of becoming what you encourage them to be, not what you nag them to be.

To disagree, one doesn't have to be disagreeable.

—*Barry Goldwater with Jack Casserly*, Goldwater
*(Doubleday)*

66

Lord, when we are wrong, make us willing to change. And when we are right, make us easy to live with.

—*Peter Marshall (1902–1949)*

We live in an age where people would rather be envied than esteemed. And when that happens, God help us.

—*Garry Trudeau (1948–    )*

Man seldom knows what he can do until he tries to undo something he did.

Men are born equal but they are also born different.

—*Erich Fromm (1900–1980)*

All mankind is divided into three classes: those that are immovable, those that are movable, and those that move.

—*Benjamin Franklin (1706–1790)*

If you're naturally kind, you attract a lot of people you don't like. *—William Feather, Sr.*

There is no genius without a mixture of madness.
*—Aristotle (384–322 B.C.)*

There are a thousand hacking at the branches of evil to one who is striking at the root. *—Henry David Thoreau (1817–1862)*

People are divided into two groups—the righteous and the unrighteous—and the righteous do the dividing.

The best index of a man's character is (a) how he treats people who can't do him any good, and (b) how he treats people who can't fight back. *—Abigail Van Buren*

Man is the only animal that blushes—or needs to.
*—Mark Twain (1835–1910)*

We are generally more persuaded by the reasons we discover ourselves than by those given to us by others.
*—Blaise Pascal (1623–1662)*

Only when we know little do we know anything; doubt grows with knowledge.
*—Johann Wolfgang von Goethe (1749–1832)*

The mind of a bigot is like the pupil of the eye; the more light you pour on it, the more it will contract.
*—Oliver Wendell Holmes, Jr. (1841–1935)*

The man who spends his life building walls instead of bridges has no right to complain if he is lonely.

There are two ways of exerting one's strength: one is pushing down, the other is pulling up.
*—Booker T. Washington (1856–1915)*

God wisely designed the human body so that we can neither pat our own backs nor kick ourselves too easily.

Most of us will never do great things, but we can do small things in a great way.

We can't all be heroes because somebody has to sit on the curb and clap as they go by.     —*Will Rogers (1879–1935)*

The worst sin towards our fellow creatures is not to hate them, but to be indifferent to them.

    —*George Bernard Shaw (1856–1950)*


If you treat an individual as he is, he will stay as he is, but if you treat him as if he were what he ought to be and could be, then he will become what he ought to be and what he could be.

    —*Johann Wolfgang von Goethe (1749–1832)*

Those who have done nothing are usually sure nothing can be done.


You can't hold a man down without staying down with him.

    —*Booker T. Washington (1856–1915)*

People who think they know it all are a pain in the neck to those of us who really do.

Man who say it cannot be done should not interrupt man doing it.     —*Chinese proverb*


He who knows not, and knows that he knows not, is a fool. Avoid him.

    He who knows not, and knows not that he knows not, is ignorant. Teach him.

    He who knows, and knows not that he knows, is asleep. Waken him.

    But he who knows, and knows that he knows, is a wise man. Follow him.

    . . . He who knows not whether he knows or knows not anything at all is a politician. Do not trust him.

    —*James P. Hogan,* Endgame Enigma

## Humor

The kind of humor I like is the thing that makes me laugh for five seconds and think for ten minutes.

*—William Davis (1909–1927)*

A sense of values and a sense of humor are inextricably related.

*—Rev. Paul Mueller, Vicar of Priests, Diocese of Toledo*

## Ideas

Ideas are very much like children—your own are wonderful.

A new idea is delicate. It can be killed by a sneer or yawn; it can be stabbed to death by a quip, and worried to death by a frown on the right man's brow.          *—Charlie Brower*

Exhilaration is that feeling you get just after a great idea hits you, and before you realize what's wrong with it.

—Changing Times, *The Kiplinger Magazine*

The sequence in the acceptance of a new idea:
1. It's a foolish idea and won't work.
2. It's not a bad idea, but the time isn't ripe.
3. The time is ripe, but we couldn't finance it.
4. I was always in favor of the idea.     —*Edgar Dale*

Charles H. Townes, who won a Nobel Prize for his work in laser technology, opened his talk with a disclaimer. "It's like the beaver told the rabbit as they stared up at the immense wall of Hoover Dam, 'No, I didn't actually build it myself. But it was based on an idea of mine.' "

Only the wise possess ideas; the greater part of mankind are possessed by them.  —*Samuel Taylor Coleridge (1722–1834)*


# Idleness

The only thing wrong with doing nothing is that you never know when you're finished.

Thank God every morning when you get up that you have something to do which must be done, whether you like it or not. Being forced to do your best, will breed in you temperance, self-control, diligence, strength of will, content, and a hundred other virtues which the idle never know.

—*Charles Kingsley (1819–1875)*

To do nothing is the way to be nothing.  —*Nathaniel Howe*

To be successful, you have to keep moving. After all, no one stumbles on something sitting down.

Shun idleness. It is a rust that attaches itself to the most brilliant of metals.     —*Voltaire (1694–1778)*

A youth was questioning a lonely old man. "What is life's heaviest burden?" he asked.

The old fellow answered sadly, "To have nothing to carry."

By too much sitting still the body becomes unhealthy, and soon the mind.     —*Henry Wadsworth Longfellow (1807–1882)*

No one is as tired as the person who does nothing.

One disadvantage of having nothing to do is that you can't stop and rest.

## Inferiority

Some men think they have an inferiority complex, when, as a matter of fact, they are just inferior.

Remember, no one can make you feel inferior without your consent. —*Eleanor Roosevelt (1884–1962)*

## Inheritance

The teary eyed widow asked the attorney about her late husband's will. "I'm sorry," he said, "but your husband left all he had to The Contented Home for Poor Widows."

"But what about me?" she asked.

"You were all he had."

—*Judge Harry T. Shafer and Angie Papadakis,* The Howls of Justice *(Harcourt Brace Jovanovich)*

The only thing of value we can give kids is what *we are,* not what *we have.*

What you have inherited from your fathers, earn over again for yourselves, or it will not be yours.

—*Johann Wolfgang von Goethe (1794–1832)*

## Innovation/Change

The dogmas of the quiet past are inadequate to the stormy present. . . . As our case is new, so we must think anew and act anew. —*Abraham Lincoln (1809–1865)*

Originality is the art of concealing your source.

Imagination is more important than knowledge. Knowledge is limited, whereas imagination embraces the entire world—stimulating progress, giving birth to evolution.

—*Albert Einstein (1879–1955)*

One must change one's tactics at least once every ten years if one wishes to maintain one's superiority.

—*Napoleon Bonaparte (1769–1821)*

"I must do something," will always solve more problems than "Something must be done."

Originality is the art of concealing your source.

Change is inevitable—except from a vending machine.

The world is changing so fast nowadays you couldn't stay wrong all the time even if you tried.

I am more of a sponge than an inventor. I absorb ideas from every source. I take half-matured schemes for mechanical development and make them practical. I am a sort of a middleman between the long-haired and impractical inventor and the hard-headed businessman who measures all things in terms of dollars and cents. My principal business is giving commercial value to the brilliant but misdirected ideas of others.

—*Thomas Edison (1847–1931)*

I was seldom able to see an opportunity until it ceased to be one. —*Mark Twain (1835–1910)*

WHAT AN IDEA WAS LIKE BEFORE EDISON

## Inventions

We owe a lot to Thomas Edison: If it wasn't for him, we'd be watching television by candlelight. —*Milton Berle (1908–   )*

Necessity may be the mother of invention, but frustration is often the father of success.

## Investments

There are two times in a man's life when he should not speculate: when he can't afford it and when he can.

—*Mark Twain (1835–1910)*

What do you need to make a small fortune on Wall Street? A large fortune.

One of the funny things about the stock market is that every time one person buys, another sells, and both think they are astute.

## Judgment

We judge ourselves by what we feel we are capable of doing, while others judge us by what we have already done.
—*Henry Wadsworth Longfellow (1807–1882)*

To have a right to do a thing is not at all the same as to be right in doing it.           —*G. K. Chesterton (1874–1936)*

## Language

Foreign language instruction helps many students become illiterate in two languages.

He was so learned that he could name a horse in nine languages; so ignorant that he bought a cow to ride on.
—*Benjamin Franklin (1706–1790)*

## Laws/Lawyers

Laws are like cobwebs, which catch small flies but let wasps and hornets break through.           —*Jonathan Swift (1667–1745)*

Man is an able creature, but he has made 35,643,692 laws and hasn't yet improved on the Ten Commandments.
—*Jacob Braude (1955–      )*

This is a court of law, young man, not a court of justice.
—*Oliver Wendell Holmes, Jr. (1841–1935)*

The law, in its majestic equality, forbids the rich as well as the poor to sleep under bridges, to beg in the streets, and to steal bread. —*Anatole France (1844–1924)*

Every man believes in trial by jury until he is called for jury duty.

Law and equity are two things which God hath joined together, but man has put asunder. —*Charles Colton (1780–1832)*

No man is above the law and no man below it.

—*Theodore Roosevelt (1858–1917)*

It is the trade of lawyers to question everything, yield nothing, and talk by the hour. —*Thomas Jefferson (1743–1826)*

A jury consists of twelve persons chosen to decide who has the better lawyer.

The love of justice in most men is only the fear of themselves suffering by injustice.

—*François de La Rochefoucauld (1613–1680)*

# Leadership

You cannot be a leader, and ask other people to follow you, unless you know how to follow, too.

—*Speaker of the House, Sam Rayburn (1882–1961)*

Leadership: The art of getting someone else to do something that you want done because he wants to do it.

—*Dwight Eisenhower (1890–1969)*

A person who follows the leader can never finish better than second.

The bass-drum player makes more noise than anybody else, but he doesn't lead the band.

When you are getting kicked in the rear, it must mean you're in front.    —*Bishop Fulton J. Sheen (1895–1979)*

Lead, follow, or get out of the way.

—*Desk slogan of Ted Turner, broadcast and sports mogul*

You can judge leaders by the size of the problems they tackle— people nearly always pick a problem their own size, and ignore or leave to others the bigger or smaller ones.

Leadership is not bestowed—it is yours only for as long as it is continuously earned.

A man who cannot lead and will not follow invariably obstructs.

We don't want to be like the leader in the French Revolution who said, "There go my people. I must find out where they are going so I can lead them."    —*John F. Kennedy (1917–1963)*

A person who can't lead and won't follow makes a dandy roadblock.

# Lies/Lying

I don't mind lying, but I hate inaccuracy.
—*Samuel Butler (1835–1902)*

He who permits himself to tell a lie once, finds it much easier to do it a second time.    —*Thomas Jefferson (1743–1826)*

All that a man gets by lying is that he is not believed when he speaks the truth.

Sin has many tools, but a lie is the handle which fits them all.
—*Oliver Wendell Holmes, Sr. (1809–1894)*

No man has a good enough memory to make a successful liar.
—*Abraham Lincoln (1809–1865)*

# Life

In spite of the cost of living, it's still popular.

Monday is an awful way to spend one-seventh of your life.

People would enjoy life more if, once they got what they wanted, they could remember how much they wanted it.

A long life may not be good enough . . . but a good life is always long enough.

Life is the childhood of our immortality.

Only a life lived for others is a life worthwhile.
                              —*Albert Einstein (1879–1955)*

Everyone has some useful purpose in life, if only to serve as a horrible example.


Life is more fun when you don't keep score.

The aim of life is to spend it for something that will outlast it.
                              —*William James (1842–1910)*

We are always getting ready to live, but never living.
                              —*Ralph Waldo Emerson (1803–1882)*


Life is like a ten-speed bike. Most of us have gears we never use.

In life, you can never do a kindness too soon because you never know how soon it will be too late.
                              —*Ralph Waldo Emerson (1803–1882)*

Nothing in life is to be feared. It is only to be understood.
                              —*Marie Curie (1867–1934)*

Life is a play; 'tis not its length, but its performance that counts.                    —*Seneca (4 B.C.–A.D. 65)*

Life is not a-having and a-getting, but a-being and a-becoming.

80

Life can be understood by looking backward, but it must be lived by looking forward.

—*Sören Aabye Kierkegaard (1813–1855)*

Begin at once to live, and count each day as a separate life.

—*Seneca (4 B.C.–A.D. 65)*

There is no cure for birth and death, save to enjoy the interval.

—*George Santayana (1863–1952)*

## Losing

Most people admire a good loser—as long as it's somebody else.

How a person plays the game shows something of his character; how he or she loses shows all of it.

# Love

Love is only the dirty trick played on us to achieve continuation of the species. —*W. Somerset Maugham (1874–1966)*

At the touch of love, everyone becomes a poet.
—*Plato (ca. 427–347 B.C.)*

We cannot know whether we love God, although there may be strong reasons for thinking so, but there can be no doubt about whether we love our neighbor or not.
—*Saint Teresa of Avila (1515–1582)*

Seeing several familiar faces here reminds me of the man who, while making love asked, "Am I the first man you ever loved?"
   She thought for a minute and replied, "You could be, your face is familiar."

Love sought is good, but given unsought is better.
—*William Shakespeare (1564–1616)*

Love is strong as death. —*Song of Solomon 8:6*

Love is not blind; it sees more, not less. But because it sees more, it is willing to see less.

Love has power to give in a moment what toil can scarcely give in an age. —*Johann Wolfgang von Goethe (1749–1832)*

Love alone is capable of uniting living beings in such a way as to complete and fulfill them, for it alone takes them and joins them by what is deepest in themselves.

Being deeply loved by someone gives you strength, while loving someone deeply gives you courage.

A man in love sees a pimple as a dimple.

—*Japanese proverb*

# Luck

You can't hope to be lucky. You have to prepare to be lucky.

The harder you work, the luckier you get.
—*Gary Player (1935–    )*

There is no one luckier than he who thinks himself so.
—*German proverb*

Chance sometimes opens the door, but luck belongs to the good players.
—*Bernard M. Baruch (1870–1965)*

If your ship doesn't come in, swim out to it!
—*Jonathan Winters (1925–    )*

## Majority

Whenever you find yourself on the side of the majority, it is time to pause and reflect.
—*Mark Twain (1835–1910)*

For everything you have lost, you have gained something else; and for everything you gain, you lose something.

—*Ralph Waldo Emerson (1803–1882)*

## Man/Men

Man is that foolish creature who tries to get even with his enemies—and ahead of his friends.

It's impossible for a woman to be married to the same man for fifty years. After the first twenty-five, he's not the same man.

By all means marry. If you get a good wife, you will become very happy; if you get a bad one, you will become a philosopher—and that is good for every man.

—*Socrates (470–399 B.C.)*

The only time a woman really changes a man is when he's a baby.          —*Natalie Wood (1938–1981)*

Some men are so macho they'll get you pregnant just so they can kill a rabbit.          —*Maureen Murphy*

## Management

The first myth of management is that it exists.

Spencer's Law of Data:
1.  Anyone can make a decision given enough facts.
2.  A good manager can make a decision without enough facts.
3.  A perfect manager can operate in perfect ignorance.

In any organization, there is always one person who really knows what's going on. That person must be fired.

General John Galvin, Supreme Allied Commander in Europe and Commander-in-Chief of U.S. European Command, was asked what it was like to be in charge of so many and varied forces. His reply: "I often feel like the director of a cemetery. I have a lot of people under me, but nobody listens."

84

Few things are quite so embarrassing as watching your boss do something you just said couldn't be done.

Soldiers win battles and generals get the credit.
—*Napoleon Bonaparte (1769–1821)*

There is no limit to what can be accomplished if it doesn't matter who gets the credit.

You can't delegate your thinking.

Anyone can hold the helm when the sea is calm.
—*Publilius Syrus (fl. 1 cent. B.C.)*

The best executive is the one who has sense enough to pick good men to do what he wants done, and self-restraint enough to keep from meddling with them while they do it.
—*Theodore Roosevelt (1858–1919)*

Men of thought should have nothing to do with action.

—*Oscar Wilde (1854–1900)*

In 1799, General Tamax received a proposal from Napoleon, who wished to enter the Russian service. They were unable to agree however, as Napoleon demanded the rank of major.

The secret of managing is to keep the guys who hate you away from the guys who are undecided.

—*Casey Stengel (1890–1975)*

I don't want any "yes-men" around me. I want everybody to tell me the truth even if it costs them their jobs.

—*Samuel Goldwyn (1882–1974)*

You can hire people to work for you, but you must win their hearts to have them work with you.

Employees like to be treated well, but they also like to be *used* well.

Never tell people how to do things. Tell them what to do and they will surprise you with their ingenuity.

—*General George Patton (1885–1945)*

When I can't handle events, I let them handle themselves.

—*Henry Ford (1863–1947)*


# Marriage

Marriage resembles a pair of scissors, so joined that they cannot be separated, often moving in opposite directions, yet always punishing anyone who comes between them.

—*Rev. Sydney Smith (1771–1845)*


Nothing flatters a man as much as the happiness of his wife; he is always proud of himself as the source of it.

—*Samuel Johnson (1709–1784)*

Marriage teaches you such important virtues as commitment, loyalty, dedication, perseverance, meekness, and many other things you wouldn't need if you had stayed single.

A successful marriage requires falling in love many times, always with the same person.

One of the greatest mysteries of life is how that idiot your daughter married can be the father of the smartest grandchildren in the whole world.

Behind every successful man is a surprised mother-in-law.

Thus grief still treads upon the heels of pleasure;
    Marry in haste, repent in leisure.

—*William Congreve (1670–1729)*

Variability is one of the virtues of a woman. It obviates the crude requirement for polygamy. If you have one good wife, you are sure to have a spiritual harem.

—*G. K. Chesterton (1874–1936)*

The most happy marriage I can picture would be the union of a deaf man to a blind woman.

—*Samuel Taylor Coleridge (1772–1834)*

In the heat of an argument, a wife exclaims to her husband, "This just goes to prove that women are smarter than men!"
    Her husband stared at her for a moment and replied, "You're right, dear, I married you and you married me."

A bride-to-be was crying to her mother, "I can't marry Joe; he is not as religious as I thought. Why, he doesn't even believe in Hell!"
    Her mother thought for a moment and replied, "Go ahead and marry him—between the two of us, we'll show him how wrong he is!"

There is no real need for stringent penalties to be placed upon convicted bigamists—after all, they have two mothers-in-law.

—*Lord Chief Justice Russell*

Marriage is a journey towards an unknown destination: The discovery that people must share not only what they don't know about each other, but what they don't know about themselves.

Only two things are necessary to keep one's wife happy. One is to let her think she is having her own way, and the other, to let her have it.                      —*Lyndon Johnson (1908–1973)*

Keep your eyes wide open before marriage, and half-shut afterwards.                      —*Benjamin Franklin (1706–1790)*

## Maturity

The mark of an immature man is that he wants to die nobly for a cause, while the mark of a mature man is that he wants to live humbly for one.                      —*Wilhelm Stekel (1868–1940)*

Maturity is the ability to do a job whether or not you are supervised, to carry money without spending it, and bear an injustice without wanting to get even.        —*Ann Landers*

Maturity begins when we're content to feel we're right about something, without feeling the necessity to prove someone else wrong.

## Medicine/Doctors

My doctor is wonderful. Once, in 1955, when I couldn't afford an operation, he touched up the X-Rays.
                                —*Joey Bishop (1918–    )*

Let no one suppose that the words doctor and patient can disguise from the parties that they are employer and employee.
                —*George Bernard Shaw (1856–1950)*

## Memory

When I face an issue of great import that cleaves both constituents and colleagues, I always take the same approach. I engage in deep deliberation and quiet contemplation. I wait to the last possible minute and then I always vote with the losers. Because, my friend, the winners never remember and the losers never forget.        —*Senator Everett Dirksen (1896–1969)*

He who receives a good turn should never forget it, and he who does one should never remember it.

## Ministers

A southern minister whose sermon had developed on the point that salvation is free—free as the water we drink—was then obliged to complain that the collection was very small that day. A member of the congregation rose to remind the minister that he had just said that salvation was as free as water. "Indeed it is," replied the minister, "but when we pipe it to you, you have to pay for the plumbing."

## Mistakes/Errors

Show me a man who doesn't make mistakes and I'll show you a man who doesn't do anything.

—*Theodore Roosevelt (1858–1917)*

The greatest mistake you can make in life is to be continually fearing you will make one.

An error doesn't become a mistake until you refuse to correct it.

Don't ever be afraid to admit you were wrong. It's like saying you're wiser today than you were yesterday.

90

A man who has committed a mistake and doesn't correct it is committing another mistake.     —*Confucius (551–479 B.C.)*

## Money

The luxury becomes the necessity if you can make the down payment on it.

Thrift is a wonderful virtue, especially in one's ancestors.

A husband walked into the house completely out of breath. "What happened, honey?" asked his wife.

"It's a great new idea I have," he gasped. "I ran all the way home behind the bus and saved 50 cents."

"Well, that certainly wasn't very bright," answered his wife. "Why didn't you run home behind a taxi and save three dollars?"     —Rotempary, *Tempe, Arizona*

God shows his contempt for wealth by the kind of person he selects to receive it.

Money is like an arm or a leg; use it or lose it.
                              —*Henry Ford (1863–1947)*

Sometimes one pays most for the things one gets for nothing.
                              —*Albert Einstein (1879–1955)*

Used to be you went without things to have money. Today, you go around without money to have things.

Money is the fruit of evil as often as the root of it.
                              —*Henry Fielding (1707–1754)*

Creditors have better memories than debtors.
                              —*Benjamin Franklin (1706–1790)*

A few years ago at the PepsiCo stockholders meeting, stockholder John Gilbert addressed Chairman Donald Kendall. "I know this is a very successful corporation and that your job is very important," he said. "But don't you think earning $800,000 a year is a little excessive for one man?"

91

The audience was silent. Kendall was quick to respond. Leaning casually on the lectern at the front of the room, he looked Gilbert in the eye. "John," he said, "I have a wife."

—*Geoffrey Thompson in White Plains, N.Y.,* Reporter Dispatch

If money is your hope for independence, you will never have it. The only real security that a man can have in this world is a reserve of knowledge, experience and ability.

—*Henry Ford (1863–1947)*

The man who would be truly happy should not study to enlarge his estate, but to contract his desires.

—*Plato (ca. 427–347 B.C.)*

"Extra" money is defined as that which you have in your possession just before the car breaks down.

Thousands upon thousands are yearly brought into a state of real poverty by their great anxiety not to be thought poor.

—*William Cobbett (1763–1835)*

Upon being notified of having bounced a check from their account, the wife shouted to her husband, *"You* say I'm overdrawn—*I* say you're underdeposited."

If your account with a credit card company gets screwed up, do not attempt to unsnarl it. It's simpler just to move away and start a new life under an assumed name.

—*Robert Stapp in Denver* Rocky Mountain News

# Morals

Morals consist of political morals, commercial morals, ecclesiastical morals, and morals.     —*Mark Twain (1835–1910)*

Cowards can never be moral.

—*Mohandas Gandhi (1869–1948)*

If moral behavior were simply following rules, we could program a computer to be moral.

I used to be Snow White, but I drifted.

—*Mae West (1893–1980)*

# Music

A wave of vulgar, filthy and suggestive music has inundated this land. Nothing but ragtime prevails, and the cakewalk with its obscene posturings, its lewd gestures. Our children, our young men and women, are continually exposed to its contiguity, to the monotonous attrition of this vulgarizing music. It is artistically and morally depressing and should be suppressed by press and pulpit.     —*Musical Courier, Sept. 13, 1899*

I don't understand anything about the ballet. All I know is that during the intervals the ballerinas stink like horses.

—*Anton Chekhov (1860–1904)*

Classical music is the kind that we keep hoping will turn into a tune. —*Kin Hubbard (1868–1930)*

Music washes away from the soul the dust of everyday life.
—*Berthold Auerbach (1812–1882)*

Jazz: Music invented by demons for the torture of imbeciles.
—*Henry van Dyke (1852–1933)*

When the kindergarten teacher returned to her class after being absent, she asked the children how they liked their substitute teacher. "She was all right," said one little boy, "but she wasn't as smart as you. She had to use two hands to play the piano."

94

# Obsolescence

The British have always been good at the patronage system. For more than twenty years, an attendant stood for no apparent reason at the foot of the stairway leading to the House of Commons. At last someone checked and discovered that the job had been held in the attendant's family for three generations. It seemed it had originated when the stairs had been painted, and the grandfather had been assigned to a patronage position to warn people not to step on the wet paint.

—*John F. Parker in* Roll Call

The British created a civil service job in 1803 calling for a man to stand on the Cliffs of Dover with a spyglass. He was supposed to ring a bell if he saw Napoleon coming. The job was abolished in 1945. —*Robert Sobel*

# Occupations

If a man is called to be streetsweeper, he should sweep streets even as Michelangelo painted, or Beethoven composed music, or Shakespeare wrote poetry. He should sweep streets so well that all the hosts of heaven and earth will pause to say, here lived a great streetsweeper who did his job well.

—*Martin Luther King, Jr. (1929–1968)*

The quality of a person's life is in direct proportion to their commitment to excellence, regardless of their chosen field of endeavor. —*Vince Lombardi (1913–1970)*


# Oops! (Famous Erroneous Predictions)

The South has too much common sense and good temper to break up the Union. —*Abraham Lincoln, 1860*

That's an amazing invention, but who would ever want to use one of them?

—*Rutherford B. Hayes, 1876, after witnessing a demonstration of the telephone*

The phonograph is of no commercial value.

—*Thomas Edison, 1880*

The cinema is little more than a fad. —*Charlie Chaplin, 1916*

Believe me, Germany is unable to wage war.

—*David Lloyd George, former Prime Minister of Great Britain, 1934*

*Gone With the Wind* is going to be the biggest flop in Hollywood history. I'm just glad it'll be Clark Gable who's falling flat on his face and not Gary Cooper. —*Gary Cooper, 1938*

The United States will not be a threat to us for decades—not in 1945 but at the earliest 1970 or 1980. —*Adolf Hitler, 1940*

No matter what happens, the United States Navy is not going to be caught napping.
—*Frank Knox, U.S. Secretary of the Navy, December 4, 1941*

I would have made a good pope. —*Richard M. Nixon, 1980*

I think there is a world market for about five computers.
—*Thomas J. Watson, Chairman of the Board of IBM, 1943*

## Opinions

Every man has a right to his opinion, but no man has the right to be wrong in his facts. —*Bernard M. Baruch (1870–1965)*

Predominant opinions are generally the opinions of the generation that is vanishing. —*Benjamin Disraeli (1804–1881)*

For the great enemy of the truth is very often not the lie—deliberate, contrived, and dishonest—but the myth—persistent, persuasive, and unrealistic. Too often we hold fast to the clichés of our forebears. We subject all facts to a pre-fabricated set of interpretations. We enjoy the comfort of our opinions without the discomfort of thought.

—*John F. Kennedy (1917–1963)*

## Optimism/Pessimism/Positive Thinking

The optimist is often as wrong as the pessimist, but he is far happier.

An optimist is the fellow who fell out of the eightieth story window of a skyscraper and as he passed the fourth floor said, "So far so good."

It takes both the sun and the rain to make a rainbow.

Pessimist—one who, when he has the choice of two evils, chooses both.                              —*Oscar Wilde (1854–1900)*

A pessimist is someone who can look at the land of milk and honey and see only calories and cholesterol.

An idealist is one who, on noticing that a rose smells better than a cabbage, concludes that it will also make better soup.
                              —*H. L. Mencken (1880–1956)*

When it is dark enough, you can see the stars.
                              —*Charles A. Beard (1874–1948)*

Sometimes the light at the end of the tunnel is an oncoming train.                  —*Notre Dame Football Coach Lou Holtz*

An optimist is a person who goes to the window every morning and says, "Good morning, God!" The pessimist goes to the window every morning and says, "Good god, morning!"

The optimist proclaims that we live in the best of all possible worlds, and the pessimist fears this is true.

# Origins

Why are so many barns painted red? In the mid-19th century, some American farmers found they could make a cheap and long-lasting wood covering from red iron oxide, skim milk, lime, and linseed oil. This mixture gave the barn a bright red color. Its use because so widespread that, by the late 1800's, red had become traditional for barns.
—*Douglas B. Smith,* Ever Wonder Why? *(Ballantine Books)*

Julius Caesar had set January 1 as the starting date for a new year, but 600 years later the church proclaimed that the Feast of the Annunciation, March 25, would henceforth mark the beginning, and for almost a thousand years this was accepted as New Year's Day. Then, in 1582, Pope Gregory XIII put it back to January 1.

99

During the Middle Ages, bakers suffered severe penalties if they were caught selling loaves of bread that were below the legal weight. To avoid prosecution for any unintentional sale below this standard, bakers added a free loaf to every 12. So, a "baker's dozen" is really 13.

—*Neil Ewart*, Everyday Phrases *(Blandford Books, Ltd.)*

## Parents/Parenting

Why is it in today's society that one father can care for ten children better than ten children can care for one father?

Diogenes struck the father when the son swore.

—*Robert Burton (1577–1640)*

The man with six kids will always be happier than the man with six million dollars, because the man with six million dollars always wants more.

When I was a boy of fourteen, my father was so ignorant I could hardly stand to have the man around. But when I got to be 21, I was astonished at how much he had learned in 7 years.
—*Mark Twain (1835–1910)*

Mixed emotions is when your teen-age son gets an A+ in sex education.

The first half of our lives is ruined by our parents and the second half by our children.     —*Clarence Darrow (1857–1938)*

By the time we realize our parents were right, we have children who think we're wrong.

A research organization, making a study of juvenile delinquency, telephoned fifty homes between 9:30 and 10:30 at night to ask parents if they knew where their children were.

Half of the calls were answered by children who had no idea where their parents were.

There are only two lasting bequests we can hope to give to our children. One of these is roots, the other, wings.

—*Hodding Carter*

You don't have to deserve your mother's love. You have to deserve your father's. He's more particular.

—*Robert Frost (1874–1963)*

## Patience/Perseverance

Persistent people begin their success where others end in failure.

Things may come to those who wait, but only the things left by those who hustle. —*Abraham Lincoln (1809–1865)*

He that can have patience can have what he will.

—*Benjamin Franklin (1706–1790)*

Adopt the peace of nature; her secret is patience.

—*Ralph Waldo Emerson (1803–1882)*

## Perfection

The pursuit of excellence is gratifying and healthy; the pursuit of perfection is frustrating, neurotic, and a terrible waste of time.

When you aim for perfection, you discover it's a moving target.

Aim at perfection in everything, though in most things it is unattainable; however, those who aim at it, and persevere, will come much nearer to it than those whose laziness and dependency make them give it up as unattainable.

—*Lord Chesterfield (1694–1773)*

A man would do nothing if he waited until he could do it so well that no one could find fault.

—*John Henry Cardinal Newman (1801–1890)*

Perfection is attained by slow degrees; it requires the hand of time.    —*Voltaire (1694–1778)*

## Perspective

An example of different perspectives: My son has just discovered the wonderful concept of inflation, which up to now is what made his balloons bigger, is also what is making his candy bars smaller.

Though the boys throw stones at the frogs in sport, yet the frogs do not die in sport but in earnest.

—*Plutarch (ca. A.D. 50–125)*

103

Sometimes, lack of perspective can lead to tragic mistakes. Consider the pilots of (XXX) Airlines last month, coincidentally the airline I flew in on today, and the problems the pilots had as a result of faulty perception. In preparing for take-off, the pilot said to the co-pilot, "My goodness, this is a short runway— you'd better give me 10% more flap to give us the lift to get up quicker." A few seconds later, the pilot again said, "Gee, this runway is REALLY short—better give me 20% more flap." The co-pilot again obliged. Upon receiving clearance for take-off, the plane began to roll and the pilot screamed, "Hurry! Give me 50% flap—we're not going to make it!" Sure enough, the plane ran off the end of the runway and crashed. The next day in the hospital, the pilot was lying in the bed and said to his roommate, the co-pilot, "I can't believe how short that runway was! I've never seen one that short!"

The co-pilot, lying in a body cast, replied, "Yeah, but did you see how WIDE it was?"

You can observe a lot by just watching.
                                        —*Yogi Berra (1925–    )*

A 747 was halfway across the Atlantic when the captain got on the loudspeaker: "Attention, passengers. We have lost one of our engines, but we can certainly reach London with the three we have left. Unfortunately, we will arrive an hour late as a result." An hour later the captain made another announcement: "Sorry, but we lost another engine. Still, we can travel on two. I'm afraid we will now arrive two hours late." Shortly thereafter, the passengers heard the captain's voice again, "Guess what, folks. We just lost our third engine, but please be assured we can fly with only one. We will now arrive in London three hours late."

At this point, one passenger became furious. "For Pete's sake," he shouted, "If we lose another engine, we'll be up here all night!"

# Philosophy

I've developed a new philosophy—I only dread one day at a time.
—*Charles Schulz (1922–    )*

There is no record in human history of a happy philosopher.
—*H. L. Mencken (1880–1956)*

Science is what you know; philosophy is what you don't know.
—*Bertrand Russell (1872–1969)*

A little philosophy inclineth a man's mind to atheism, but depth in philosophy bringeth men's minds about to religion.
—*Francis Bacon (1561–1626)*

A true philosopher never argues. He mentally concludes that his opponent is an ass, and keeps his mouth shut.

# Planning/Direction

"Would you tell me, please, which way I ought to go from here?"

"That depends a good deal on where you want to go to," said the Cat.

"I don't much care where," said Alice.

"Then it doesn't matter which way you go," said the Cat.

—*Lewis Carroll*, Alice in Wonderland

There is a time when we must firmly choose the course which we will follow or the endless drift of events will make the decision for us.           —*Herbert V. Prochnow*

When other people take a long time to do something, they're slow. When we take a long time, we're through.

Most people don't plan to fail—they fail to plan.

Where there is no vision, people perish.         —*Proverbs 29:18*

The first 90% of the task takes 90% of the time; the last 10% of the task takes the other 90% of the time.

You can never tell which way the train went by looking at the track.

Every one minute you spend in planning will save you at least three minutes in execution.

—*Crawford Greenwald, Chairman of Board, E.I. DuPont*

There are only three types of people: those who make things happen, those who watch things happen, and those who say, "What happened?"

So then, we must always aim at those things that bring peace and that help strengthen one another.         —*Romans 14:9*

You must have long-range goals to keep you from being frustrated by short-term failures.         —*Charles C. Noble*

106

If you tell people where to go, but not how to get there, you'll be amazed at the results.

*—General George Patton (1885–1945)*

The six phases of project development:
1. Wild enthusiasm
2. Disillusionment
3. Total confusion
4. Search for the guilty
5. Punishment of the innocent
6. Promotion of non-participants

On a plane bound for Europe, the pilot's voice suddenly came over the public address system: "Ladies and gentlemen, I have two pieces of news for you. One of them is good, and one of them is not so good. The bad news is that we are hopelessly lost—I don't have any idea of where we are. But, as I told you, there's good news, too. The good news is that we have a 200 mile-an-hour tailwind and we're making great time." (Use this story with any topic where change is important, e.g. "We may not know where we're going, but we're getting there awfully fast.")

The speed of a runaway horse counts for nothing.

*—Jean Cocteau (1889–1963)*

It is more important to know where you are going than to get there quickly. Do not mistake activity for achievement.

*—Mabel Newcomber*

Trying to achieve an implementation date, I am reminded of a young lad who rushed breathlessly up to the train platform just as the last car pulled away. A man standing nearby, observing the incident, smiled sympathetically at the boy. "I guess you did not run fast enough," he said.

"Oh, yes I did," the boy responded, courteously but firmly. "I just didn't start soon enough."

If you think you're confused, think of poor Columbus. He didn't know where he was going when he started. When he got there, he didn't know where he was, and when he got back, he didn't know where he had been—and he did it all on borrowed money. Today, he's a hero.

The last thing one knows is what to put first.

—*Blaise Pascal (1623–1662)*

Some years ago, the British House of Commons was interrupted by the news that after years of effort and millions of dollars, the cable to Africa had been completed. After the hurrahs and hat-tossing died down, Winston Churchill rose to say, "Excellent, excellent. Now, what shall we tell the Africans?"

All too often in planning, I can see evidence of a philosophy similar to a slip-up made by a prosecuting attorney in summing up his case to the jury: "And those, ladies and gentlemen, are the conclusions on which I base my facts."

A task without a vision is drudgery; a vision without a task is a dream; but a task with a vision is ecstasy.

One does not plan and then try to make circumstances fit those plans. One tries to make plans fit the circumstances.

—*General George Patton (1885–1945)*

## Pleasure

If you resolve to give up smoking, drinking, and loving, you don't actually live longer; it just seems longer.

To err is human, but it feels divine.

—*Mae West (1893–1980)*

## Point of View

A man, whose father was hanged, when asked how his father met his death, replied that he died at a public function when the platform gave way.

108

If you steal from one author, it's plagiarism; if you steal from twenty authors, it's research.

The girl who can't dance says the band can't play.

—*Yiddish proverb*

Perception is selective: A bald man sees non-bald men as abnormally hairy.

There is a fine difference of perspective between getting involved and being committed. In ham and eggs, the chicken is involved but the pig is committed.

—*John-Allen Price*, The Pursuit of the Phoenix
*(Kensington)*

To a worm, digging in the hard ground is more relaxing than going fishing.

# Political Parties

Some men change their party for the sake of their principles; others their principles for the sake of their party.
—*Winston Churchill (1874–1965)*

I am not a member of any organized political party—I am a Democrat.
—*Will Rogers (1879–1935)*

While the Republicans are smart enough to make money, the Democrats are smart enough to get into office every two or three times a century to take it away from them.
—*Will Rogers (1879–1935)*

Republicans sleep in twin beds—some even in separate rooms. That is why there are more Democrats.
—*Walt Stanton (1914–    )*

The more you read about politics, the more you got to admit that each party is worse than the other.
—*Will Rogers (1879–1935)*

A conservative is someone who admires radicals a century after they're dead.

The modern conservative is engaged in one of man's oldest exercises in moral philosophy, that is the search for a superior moral justification for selfishness.
—*John Kenneth Galbraith (1908–    )*

A conservative is someone who believes in reform. But not now.

A liberal is one who has both feet planted firmly in the air.
—*Adlai Stevenson (1900–1965)*

I can remember back when a liberal was one who was generous with his own money.
—*Will Rogers (1879–1935)*

A man of 90 years old, a staunch Republican all his life, was experiencing failing health. When his doctor confirmed the end

110

was not far off, he asked his son to take him to the courthouse so he could change his voter registration from Republican to Democrat. The young man protested, and reminded his father of the leadership positions he held in the Republican party and his strong party feelings. Finally, the old man replied to his son's scolding, "Son, if someone has to die, it might as well be one of them."

—*Larry Wilde*, More: The Official Democrat-Republican Joke Book *(Pinnacle)*

I have been thinking that I would like to make a proposition to my Republican friends . . . that if they would stop telling lies about the Democrats, we will stop telling the truth about them.

—*Adlai Stevenson (1900–1965)*

There is no distinctly native American criminal class except Congress.                     —*Mark Twain (1835–1910)*

# Politicians

Politicians are the same all over. They promise to build a bridge even when there is no river.

—*Nikita Khrushchev (1894–1971)*

You've got to be an optimist to be a Democrat, and you've got to be a humorist to stay one.     —*Will Rogers (1879–1935)*

Since a politician never believes what he says, he is surprised when others believe him.   —*Charles de Gaulle (1890–1970)*

Greater love hath no man than this, that he lay down his friends for his political life.

When they call the roll in the Senate, the senators do not know whether to answer "present" or "not guilty."

—*Theodore Roosevelt (1858–1917)*

A politician is a man who understands government and it takes a politician to run a government. A statesman is a politician who's been dead for fifteen years.

—*Harry S Truman (1884–1972)*

He knows nothing; he thinks he knows everything—that clearly points to a political career.

—*George Bernard Shaw (1856–1950)*

More men have been elected between sundown and sunup than ever were elected between sunup and sundown.

—*Will Rogers (1879–1935)*

I have come to the conclusion that politics is too serious a matter to be left to the politicians.

—*Charles de Gaulle (1890–1970)*

He is the kind of politician who would cut down a redwood tree and then mount the stump to make a speech for conservation.

—*Adlai Stevenson (referring to Richard Nixon)*

112

Mothers all want their sons to grow up to be President, but they don't want them to become politicians in the process.

—*John F. Kennedy (1917–1963)*

## Politics

As an example of illustrating that "pro" is the opposite of "con," the student offered, "Progress and Congress."

When we got into office, the thing that surprised me most was to find out that things were just as bad as we'd been saying they were. —*John F. Kennedy (1917–1963)*

I have just received the following telegram from my generous Daddy. It says, "Dear Jack: Don't buy a single more vote than is necessary. I'll be damned if I'm going to pay for a landslide.

—*John F. Kennedy (1917–1963)*

113

Politics: The gentle art of getting votes from the poor and campaign funds from the rich, by promising to protect each from the other. —*Oscar Ameringer*

Nothing is politically right which is morally wrong.
—*Thomas Jefferson (1743–1826)*

I'll tell you what the difference between capitalism and communism is. With capitalism, man exploits man; with communism it's the other way around.
—*James P. Hogan*, Endgame Enigma

Politics is a funny business. One week you're on the cover of *Time* and the next week you're doing it.

Whenever a man has cast a longing eye on offices, a rottenness begins in his conduct. —*Thomas Jefferson (1743–1826)*

An empty stomach is not a good political advisor.
—*Albert Einstein (1879–1955)*

Politics are almost as exciting as war, and quite as dangerous. In war you can only be killed once, but in politics many times.
—*Winston Churchill (1874–1965)*

Being in politics is like being a football coach. You have to be smart enough to understand the game and stupid enough to think it's important. —*Eugene McCarthy (1916–    )*

## Possessions

That which you cannot give away, you do not possess. It possesses you.

Watch out and guard yourselves from every kind of greed; because a person's true life is not made up of the things he owns. —*Luke 12:15*

I have learned to be satisfied with what I have.

—*Apostle Paul*

114

# Prayer

A grandfather overheard his granddaughter repeating the alphabet in reverent, hushed tones. "What are you doing?" he finally asked.

"I'm praying, Grandpa," she said. "I can't think of the right words, so I just say all the letters. God will put them together for me, 'cause He knows what I'm thinking."

*—Robert E. Goodrich,* What's It All About?

Serving God is doing good to man, but praying is thought an easier service and therefore more generally chosen.

*—Benjamin Franklin (1706–1790)*

The hands that help are holier than the lips that pray.

*—Robert G. Ingersoll (1833–1899)*

A major flood was devastating a southern town and all the townspeople were urged to flee their homes. One devoutly religious man refused to leave. As the water rose, a jeep was barely making it through but stopped at the man's house to ask him to get in before the flood worsened. The man declined, insisting that he had faith in the Lord and the Lord would save him. A while later, the water rose even higher and he was forced to the second story of his home. A boat came by and asked him to get in so they could flee the area. Again, he reiterated his faith in the Lord and stayed. Still later, as the water continued to rise, he was forced to take refuge on the roof of his house. A helicopter came by and lowered a ladder, but again the man refused to leave, citing his faith in the Lord. Not long thereafter, the water rose higher and the man drowned. When he reached his Maker, he immediately blurted out, "Lord, I had complete faith in You to save me, but you didn't! You ignored my prayers for help!"

The Lord looked at the man with a little disbelief and said, "What do you mean I ignored your prayers for help. . . . I sent a jeep, a boat, and a helicopter, didn't I?"

What men usually ask God when they pray is that two and two not make four.

Lord, give us enough temptation to make us tolerant,
    enough failure to make us humble,
    enough success to make us striving,
    enough tears to make us tender, and
    enough sorrow to make us sympathetic.

Do not ask to have your life's load lightened,
    But for courage to endure.
Do not ask for fulfillment in all your life,
    But for patience to accept frustration.
Do not ask for perfection in all you do,
    But for the wisdom not to repeat mistakes.
And finally, do not ask for more,
    Before saying "Thank You"
    for what you have already received.        —*Brenda Short*

116

Make me chaste and continent, but not just yet.

*—Saint Augustine (354–430)*

If radio's slim fingers can pluck a melody out of the night and toss it over mountains and sea; if the petal-white notes from a violin are blown across the desert and the city's din; if songs, like crimson roses, are caught from thin blue air—why should mortals wonder if God hears prayer?

*—Marvin Drake in* Catholic Digest

Any concern too small to be turned into a prayer is too small to be made into a burden.

Lord, I confess I am not what I ought to be, but I thank You, Lord, that I'm not what I used to be.

*—Maxie Dunnam in* The Sanctuary for Lent *(Abingdon)*

There is a vast difference between saying prayers and praying.

An elderly man was in the habit when entering church, of bowing his head on the back of the pew in front of him for a long time. This excited the interest of a youngster who asked him just what he did during that time. The old man replied, "Lad, that's a fair question and demands a fair answer. I don't know what other people do when they bow their heads, but I always count to forty!"

I have been driven many times to my knees by the overwhelming conviction that I had nowhere else to go. My own wisdom, and that of all about me seemed insufficient for the day.

*—Abraham Lincoln (1809–1865)*

I have lived to thank God that all my prayers have not yet been answered.

# Preaching

Bishop Fulton J. Sheen received an award for his television program, and like all modest recipients wished to thank those who had a part in it. He walked up to the microphone and said,

"I also want to pay tribute to my four writers: Matthew, Mark, Luke, and John."

The test of a preacher is that his congregation goes away saying not "What a lovely sermon," but "I will do something!"
—*St. Francis de Sales (1567–1622)*

A shrewd pastor began his sermon, "Folks, the subject of my sermon today is 'Liars.' As a biblical reference, how many have read what the Bible says on this subject in the sixty-ninth chapter of Matthew?" Nearly every hand in the congregation went up immediately. "That's right," said the reverend. "You're just the folks I want to preach to. There is no sixty-ninth chapter of Matthew."

There is not the least use preaching to anyone unless you chance to catch them ill.  —*Rev. Sydney Smith (1771–1845)*

118

After a preacher died and went to heaven, he noticed that a New York cabdriver had been given a higher place then he had. "I don't understand," he complained to St. Peter. "I devoted my entire life to my congregation."

"Our policy is to reward results," explained St. Peter. "Now, what happened, Reverend, whenever you gave a sermon?" The minister admitted that some in the congregation fell asleep.

"Exactly," said St. Peter. "And when people rode in this man's taxi, they not only stayed awake, they *prayed.*"

—*Raymond A. Heit in* Reader's Digest

*Reprinted with permission from the January 1990* Reader's Digest. *Copyright © 1990 by The Reader's Digest Assn., Inc.*

The rabbi came home from the synagogue looking very tired, and his wife was concerned. "What was it that you spoke about that took so much out of you?" she asked.

"I argued that it was the duty of the rich Jews to provide for the poor on Passover."

"Did you convince the congregation?" his wife asked.

"I would say," returned the rabbi, "that it was about fifty-fifty. I convinced the poor."

After a long, dry sermon, the minister announced there would be a brief meeting of the board immediately after services. To the surprise of the minister, a stranger walked up after the service, to whom the minister said, "I'm sorry, you must have misunderstood—this meeting is only for the board."

"So I heard," replied the stranger, "and if there was anyone here more bored than I am, I'd like to meet him."

A man who had lost his hat decided the simplest way to replace it was to go to the cloakroom of a church and steal one during the services. Once inside, he heard a sermon on the Ten Commandments. Coming out, he was greeted by the minister and said to him, "I want you to know, Reverend, that you have saved me from crime. I came in here with sin in my heart. I was

119

going to steal a hat, but after hearing your sermon, I changed my mind."

Flattered, the minister asked, "What in particular did I say that convinced you to change your mind?"

"Well, Reverend, when you got to the part about 'Thou shalt not commit adultery', I suddenly remembered where I left my hat!"

## Predictions

The rule of staying alive as a forecaster is to give 'em a number or give 'em a date, but never give 'em both at once.

—*Jane Bryant Quinn*

These days, you never know what's going to happen next. Ergo, eat your dessert first.

A man visited a fortuneteller and sat down in front of her crystal ball. "I see you are the father of two children," she said.

"That's what you think," the man replied. "I'm the father of three children."

The fortuneteller smiled and said, "That's what *you* think."

## Pride

Temper is what gets most of us into trouble, but pride is what keeps us there.

Pride leads to destruction, and arrogance to downfall.
—*Proverbs 16:18*

## Principles

It is often easier to fight for principles than to live up to them.
—*Adlai Stevenson (1900–1965)*

A people that values its privileges above its principles soon loses both.      —*Dwight Eisenhower (1890–1969)*

We may be personally defeated, but our principles never.
—*William Lloyd Garrison (1805–1879)*

## Problems

If all you have is a hammer, everything looks like a nail.

Once you open a can of worms, the only way to re-can them is to use a larger can.

Again and again the impossible problem is solved when we see that the problem is only a tough decision waiting to be made.
—*Robert Schuller (1926–      )*

Nothing is impossible for the man who doesn't have to do it himself.

There is nothing so small it can't be blown out of proportion.

Many a problem will solve itself if you'll forget it and go fishing.

An old Russian fable tells us of a small bird freezing to death on a country road in Russia. A peasant came along, saw the dying bird, and thought to himself, "If only I had something—anything—in which to wrap this bird, I might save its life, for surely it is freezing to death." But, unfortunately, he had nothing on him that he could spare. Nearby he caught sight of some cow droppings, and he thought in desperation, "Perhaps if I wrap the bird in that, it will warm it up enough to save is life." He picked up the bird, wrapped it in the cow dung, laid it gently on the ground, and went on his way. Sure enough, the dung began to warm the bird, and it started coming to life again. The bird felt so overjoyed at feeling warm again that it began to chirp. Just then, a starving cat wandered by and was attracted to the sound of the bird, and carefully scraping away the unique "bird-house," grabbed the bird and ate it. There are three morals to this fable. First, it's not always your enemies who put you in "it." Second, it's not always your friends who get you out of "it." Third, when you're in "it" over your head, for God's sake, don't sing!

The way I look at it, if you want the rainbow, you gotta put up with the rain. —*Dolly Parton*

One of the nice things about problems is that a good many of them do not exist except in our imaginations.

—*Steve Allen*, How to Make a Speech (*McGraw-Hill*)

If all our misfortunes were laid in one common heap, whence everyone must take an equal portion, most people would be contented to take their own and depart.

—*Socrates* (ca. 470–399 B.C.)

There is always an easy solution to every human problem: neat, plausible, and wrong. —*H. L. Mencken (1880–1956)*

A problem well stated is a problem half solved.

—*Charles Kettering (1876–1958)*

## Procrastination

Never put off till tomorrow what can be put off till day-after-tomorrow just as well.        *—Mark Twain (1835–1910)*

Old procrastinators never die; they just keep putting it off.

Today is the tomorrow you worried about yesterday.

Never do today what you can do as well tomorrow because something may occur to make you regret your premature action.        *—Aaron Burr (1756–1836)*

## Progress

I walk slowly, but I never walk backwards.
        *—Abraham Lincoln (1809–1865)*

All progress is based upon the universal innate desire on the part of every organism to live beyond its income.

*—Samuel Butler (1835–1902)*

Progress might have been all right once, but it's gone on too long now. *—Ogden Nash (1902–1971)*

Always remember that the soundest way to progress in any organization is to help the man ahead of you get promoted.

The reasonable man adapts himself to the world; the unreasonable one persists in trying to adapt the world to himself. Therefore all progress depends upon the unreasonable man.

*—George Bernard Shaw (1856–1950)*

Lenin, Stalin, and Gorbachev were riding on a train. When it came to a halt, the engineer said, "Our engine has failed—what shall I do?"

"Let the invincible spirit of the people pull us on!" Lenin declared.

"Shoot the engineer!" offered Stalin.

And Gorbachev suggested, "Close the shades and we can *pretend* were moving forward!"

All progress is the result of change, but all change is not necessarily progress.

## Publication

Only one thing is impossible for God: to find any sense in any copyright law on the planet.     —*Mark Twain (1835–1910)*

What a good thing Adam had—when he said a good thing, he knew nobody had said it before. —*Mark Twain (1835–1910)*

## Quality/Quality Control

Quality is remembered long after price is forgotten.
 —*Desk slogan of Stanley Marcus, merchandising consultant*

## Recreation

Since three-fourths of the earth's surface is water and one-fourth is land, it's clear that the good Lord intended a man should spend three times as much fishing as he does plowing.

All men are equal before fish. —*Herbert Hoover (1874–1964)*

When a man wantonly destroys one of the works of man we call him a vandal. When he wantonly destroys one of the works of God we call him a sportsman.

                    —*Joseph Wood Kurtch,* The Great Chain of Life
                    *(Houghton-Mifflin)*

I like long walks, especially when they are taken by people who annoy me.                    —*Fred Allen (1894–1956)*

Running is to walking what singing is to talking.

If there is larceny in a person, golf will bring it out.

Saint Peter halted a man at the entrance to heaven. "You've told too many lies to be permitted in here," he said.

"Have a heart," replied the man. "Remember, you were once a fisherman yourself."

Nothing increases the size of a fish like fishing all by yourself.

There's a fine line between fishing and standing on the shore like an idiot.

# Religion

It is the test of a good religion whether you can make a joke about it.                                    —*G. K. Chesterton (1874–1936)*

With a good conscience our only sure reward, with history the final judge of our deeds, let us go forth to lead the land we love, asking His blessing and His help, but knowing that here on earth God's work must truly be our own.

—*John F. Kennedy (1917–1963)*

The proverb says that Providence protects children and idiots. This is really true. I know because I have tested it.

—*Mark Twain (1835–1910)*

The Bible is like a telescope; it is not to look at but to look through.


Three couples met their deaths in a tragic accident and were standing in front of the Pearly Gates. St. Peter said to the first man, "It is true that you did many noble deeds, but you also drank a lot. You loved booze so much you even married a woman named Sherry. I think I'll send you to purgatory for a few centuries, then we'll consider your case."

The second man then told St. Peter how he was a good family man and attended church every Sunday. St. Peter

126

responded, "Yes, but you were also a miser. You loved money so much that you even married a woman named Penny. You'll have to spend some time in purgatory, too."

The third man, instead of telling St. Peter his virtues, turned around and just started walking down the path to Purgatory, calling after him to his wife, "Come on, Fanny."

—*Charleston, W. Va.* Gazette

Leopards break into the temple and drink the sacrificial chalices dry; this occurs repeatedly, again and again. Finally it can be reckoned upon beforehand and becomes part of the ceremony.
—*Franz Kafka (1883–1924)*

Many might go to heaven with half the labor they go to Hell.
—*Ben Jonson (1572–1637)*

The various modes of worship which prevailed in the Roman world were all considered by the people as equally true; by the philosopher as equally false; and by the magistrate as equally useful. —*Edward Gibbon (1737–1794)*

Fanaticism in religion is the alliance of the passions she condemns with the dogmas she professes.
—*Lord Acton (1834–1902)*

He who created us without our help will not save us without our consent. —*Saint Augustine (354–430)*

I walked today through the slums of life . . . Down the dark streets of wretchedness and of pain. I trod where few have trod, and as I walked, I challenged God. I saw the evils in the barrooms, I saw the prostitutes on the street corners. I saw men and women devoid of life . . . living in worlds of sin . . . and above the din I whispered, "Why, God, Why?"

I walked today down the lanes of hate, hearing the jeers of bitter men, hearing the names as they cursed and spat . . . "Nigger," "Kike," "Redneck." I saw the dejected men they stoned. I felt the anguish of their cries. I saw them as they slapped the lonely, as they turned their backs on human needs. Snarling, growling were these fiends from Hell, these, God called His sons! Gasping for air, I cried, "WHY, GOD, WHY?"

I walked today over war's grim dregs . . . over fields of blood, over graveless men. I saw the dead, the suffering, and the dying. I saw the pain, the waste, and I heard their screams for mercy. I saw the children gathered around, naked, hungry, diseased. The ruins, the agony, the despair! Blinded with tears, I fled down the streets and shouted, "WHY, GOD, WHY?"

"Why do you let men sin, hate, and suffer? Unmerciful Father! God, art thou blind? Art thou wicked and cruel? God, cannot You see and yet You do nothing? Why must this be?"

The world grew silent. I awaited reply. The silence was heavy. I started to tremble. I waited long—half fearing. Then, I heard close behind me, "Why, man, why?"

Men never do evil so completely and cheerfully as when they do it from religious conviction.  —*Blaise Pascal (1623–1662)*

Many have quarrelled over religion that never practiced it.
                                        —*Benjamin Franklin (1706–1790)*

One of the best tests of religion is to find yourself in church with nothing less than a 20-dollar bill in your wallet.

What God lacks is conviction—stability of character. He ought to be a Presbyterian or a Catholic or *something*—not try to be everything.                     —*Mark Twain (1835–1910)*

Religion is a journey, not a destination.

It often happens that I wake at night and begin to think about a serious problem and decide I must tell the Pope about it. Then I wake up completely and remember that I *am* the Pope.
                                        —*Pope John XXIII (1881–1963)*

A gentle Quaker, hearing a strange noise in the house one night, got up and discovered a burglar busily at work. He went up and got his gun, came back and stood quietly in the doorway. "Friend," he said, "I would do thee no harm for the world, but thou standest where I am about to shoot."

From silly devotions and from sour-faced saints, good Lord, deliver us.                    —*Saint Teresa of Avila (1515–1582)*

. . . and the Pope said, "My brothers, I bring you good news and I bring you bad news. The good news is that I have just received a phone call from Christ, who has returned to earth. The bad news is that He was calling from Salt Lake City.
                              —*Monsignor Geno Baroni*

Religion is what keeps the poor from murdering the rich.
                              —*Napoleon Bonaparte (1769–1821)*

## Religious Study

A young boy on a Sunday morning asked his father, "Dad, did you go to Sunday School when you were a little boy?"
     "I sure did. Never missed a Sunday," replied the father smugly.
     "There now, Mother, don't you see? It won't do me any good either."

One morning, a Sunday-school teacher asked her group if they knew who defeated the Philistines. After a few moments of silence, one youngster finally asked, "They're not in the NBA, are they?"

At a workshop session at our regional church convention, a seminar leader was trying to impress us with how Christian values can be applied to everyday life. For each simple example of common situations, the instructor was able to cite a parable or Bible quotation that seemed to fit the situation in modern day society. Near the end of the session, the situation given for us to react to was a common occurrence: You are driving down the road and another motorist abruptly cuts you off. When asked what would be the proper Christian response to this situation, one woman quickly responded, "Turn the other fender?"

After lecturing her six-year-old son on the golden rule, the mother concluded, "Always remember that we are in this world to help others."

The youngster mulled over this for a minute and asked, "What are the others here for?"

## Repentance/Forgiveness

The sinning is the best part of repentance. —*Arabic proverb*

If I die, I forgive you; if I recover, we shall see.

—*Spanish proverb*

In this era of rapid change, one thing remains constant: It's easier to pray for forgiveness than to resist temptation.

Many promising reconciliations have broken down because, while both parties came prepared to forgive, neither party was prepared to be forgiven.

Always forgive your enemies; nothing annoys them as much.
—*Oscar Wilde (1854–1900)*

Forgive your enemies, but never forget their names.
—*John F. Kennedy (1917–1963)*

Definition of confession: the acknowledgment made to a priest of a sinful act committed by a friend, neighbor, or acquaintance, and to which you reacted with righteous indignation.
—*Ambrose Bierce*, The Devil's Dictionary, *1911*

Most of us can forgive and forget; we just don't want the other person to forget that we forgave.

The weak can never forgive. Forgiveness is the attribute of the strong.        —*Mohandas Gandhi (1869–1948)*

The Rule of the Jesuit: It is much easier to ask for forgiveness than to ask for permission.

Forgiveness is man's deepest need and highest achievement.

Apologizing is a very desperate habit—one that is rarely cured. Nine times out of ten, the first thing a man's companion knows of his shortcomings is from his apology. It is mighty presumptuous on your part to suppose your small failures of so much consequence that you must talk about them.
—*Oliver Wendell Holmes, Sr. (1809–1894)*

# Retirement

The problem with retirement is that you can't leave all your problems at the office.

A bit of advice for those about to retire: If you're only 65, never move to a retirement community. Everybody else is in their 70's, 80's, or 90's, so whenever something has to be moved, lifted, or loaded, they yell, "Get the kid!"

## Self-Control

Self-discipline is when your conscience tells you to do something and you don't talk back.

There never has been, and cannot be, a good life without self-control. —*Leo Tolstoy (1828–1910)*

No man is fit to command another who cannot command himself. —*William Penn (1644–1718)*

For a man to conquer himself is the first and noblest of all victories. —*Plato (ca. 428–348 B.C.)*

No man is free who cannot control himself.

> —*Pythagoras (ca. 580–500 B.C.)*

The only discipline that lasts is self-discipline.
> —*Bum Phillips, former NFL coach of the Houston Oilers*

## Self-Image

Know thyself? If I knew myself, I'd run away.
> —*Johann Wolfgang von Goethe (1749–1832)*

You have no idea what a poor opinion I have of myself, and how little I deserve it. —*William S. Gilbert (1836–1911)*

Everyone thinks of changing humanity, but no one thinks of changing himself. —*Leo Tolstoy (1829–1910)*

People seldom improve when they have no other model but themselves to copy after. —*Oliver Goldsmith (1730–1774)*

For it is when the Lord thinks well of a person that he is really approved, and not when he thinks well of himself.
> —*II Corinthians 10:18*

To dream of the person you would like to be is to waste the person you are.

A conviction is that commendable quality in ourselves which we call bull-headedness in others.

Do not wish to be anything but what you are, and try to be that perfectly. —*St. Francis de Sales (1567–1622)*

All the wonders you seek are within yourself.
> —*Sir Thomas Browne (1605–1682)*

No matter where you go you can't get away from yourself, so you'd better make yourself into somebody worthwhile.

To thine own self be true, and it must follow, as the night the day, thou canst not then be false to any man.
> —*William Shakespeare (1564–1616)*

Our self-image and our habits tend to go together. Change one and you will automatically change the other.

Every new adjustment is a crisis in self-esteem.

Good breeding consists in concealing how much we think of ourselves and how little we think of the other person.

—*Mark Twain (1835–1910)*

Be yourself, and be the person you hope to be.

—*Robert Louis Stevenson (1850–1894)*

We judge ourselves by our motives and others by their actions.

—*Dwight Morrow (1873–1931)*

## Selfishness

Two men were bitter rivals. An angel was sent to rectify the

situation and appeared to one of the men and said, "You are very bitter and cold and cruel to a man who should be your friend. To cure you, the Good Lord has promised to give you one of anything in the world, if you will let your rival have two of them."

The man thought about the proposition carefully. "You mean, if I ask for one lavish, expensive house, he will get two houses?"

"Yes," replied the angel.

"And if I ask for a million dollars, he will get two million?"

"That's right," replied the angel.

"Then, I'll take one glass eye."

## Silence

Blessed is the man who, having nothing to say, abstains from giving us worthy evidence of that fact.

—*George Eliot (1819–1880)*

I have noticed that nothing I never said ever did me any harm.

—*Calvin Coolidge (1872–1933)*

When Hitler attacked the Jews, I was not a Jew, therefore, I was not concerned. And when Hitler attacked the Catholics, I was not a Catholic, and therefore, I was not concerned. And when Hitler attacked the unions and the industrialists, I was not a member of the unions and I was not concerned. Then, Hitler attacked me and the Protestant church, and there was nobody left to be concerned.

—*Martin Niemöller, 1945 (Stuttgart Statement of Guilt)*

It is better to be silent and be considered a fool than to speak and remove all doubt.

Silence is one of the hardest arguments to refute.

Teach your child to hold his tongue; he'll learn fast enough to speak. —*Benjamin Franklin (1706–1790)*

136

Silence is the ultimate weapon of power.

—*Charles de Gaulle (1890–1970)*

The difference between a successful career and a mediocre one sometimes consists of leaving about four or five things a day unsaid.

When the eagles are silent, the parrots begin to jabber.

—*Winston Churchill (1874–1965)*

# Sports

Sports is the toy department of human life.

—*Howard Cosell (1918–    )*

One man practicing sportsmanship is far better than 50 preaching it.          —*Knute Rockne (1888–1931)*

Sports do not build character. They reveal it.

—*Heywood Broun (1888–1939)*

If you aren't fired with enthusiasm, you'll be fired with enthusiasm.          —*Vince Lombardi (1913–1970)*

When you win, nothing hurts.    —*Joe Namath (1943–    )*

Old quarterbacks never die; they just pass away.

Long-distance running is 90% mental and the other half physical.

Sign at foot of ski slope: Laws of Gravity Strictly Enforced.

The race is not always to the swift, nor the battle to the strong—but that's the way to bet.

—*Damon Runyon (1884–1946)*

There are people who end up on third base and think they hit a triple to get there.          —*Barry Switzer*

If the human body recognized agony and frustration, people would never run marathons, have babies, or play baseball.

—*Carlton Fisk*

While visiting St. Patrick's Cathedral in New York and admiring the glorious architecture, I overheard a parent telling a youngster near the altar, "And under here is the place where all the cardinals are buried."

The youngster looked up in amazement and asked with great wonder, "You mean the whole team?"

Hurt is in your mind.    —*Harry Lombardi, to his son Vince*

Ability is the art of getting credit for all the home runs somebody else hits.    —*Casey Stengel (1890–1975)*

Don't let the fear of striking out hold you back.

—*Babe Ruth (1895–1948)*

I'm throwing twice as hard as I ever did. The ball's just not getting there as fast.    —*Lefty Gomez, pitcher, N.Y. Yankees*

138

I guess more players lick themselves than are ever licked by an opposing team. The first thing any man has to know is how to handle himself.                    —*Connie Mack (1862–1956)*

Football is not a contact sport. It's a collision sport. Dancing is a good example of a contact sport.
                    —*Duffy Daugherty, former Michigan State University Coach*

Praise should be directed at the performance and not the person.

Umpire Bill Guthrie, after a rookie threw his bat into the air to protest a called strike: "Son, if that bat comes down, you're out of the game."

Practice is the best of all instructors.
                    —*Publilius Syrus (fl. 1st century B.C.)*

Only in sports do we keep the temperamental, explosive employee and fire the boss.

Nobody roots for Goliath.   —*Wilt Chamberlain (1936–    )*

Just before the Notre Dame–Miami college football game in November, University of Miami's chaplain, Father Leo Armbrust, had a discussion with Notre Dame Coach Lou Holtz. During his invocation at the booster luncheon, Armbrust assured his audience that the Almighty was impartial. When Holtz got up to speak, he agreed with Father Leo. "I don't think God cares who wins tomorrow, either," said Holtz. "But His mother does."      —*Austin Murphy in* Sports Illustrated

## Statistics

Statistics are like ladies of the night. Once you get them down, you can do anything with them. —*Mark Twain (1835–1910)*

It is important to remember that figures and statistics can be misleading. We all know about the man who drowned trying to walk across a lake with an average depth of three feet.

Torture numbers, and they'll confess to anything.

There are three kinds of lies: lies, damned lies, and statistics.
—*Benjamin Disraeli (1804–1881)*

With all of the facts and figures quoted on the news and elsewhere daily, here are a few upbeat statistics: 224 million people in the United States will NOT be arrested this year; 101 million will NOT file for divorce; 58 million students will NOT riot or petition for anything; and 123 million women will not go on diets.

Many use statistics as a drunken man uses a lamp post—for support rather than illumination.

Statistics are no substitute for judgment.
—*Henry Clay (1777–1852)*

# Success

Success comes to those who are too busy to look for it.

Applause waits on success.

*—Benjamin Franklin (1706–1790)*

Success is getting what you want—happiness is wanting what you get.

There aren't any rules to success that will work unless you do.

Success is one percent inspiration and ninety-nine percent perspiration. *—Benjamin Franklin (1706–1790)*

Success is counted sweetest by those who never succeed.

*—Emily Dickinson (1830–1886)*

When success turns a person's head, he is facing failure.

Men's best successes come after their disappointments.

>—*Henry Ward Beecher (1813–1887)*

Nothing succeeds like one's own successor.

Victory belongs to the most persevering.

>—*Napoleon Bonaparte (1769–1821)*

Success is a journey, not a destination.

All you need in this life is ignorance and confidence, and then success is sure. —*Mark Twain (1835–1910)*

Try not to become a person of success but rather a person of value. —*Albert Einstein (1879–1955)*

The worst part of having success is to try finding someone who is happy for you. —*Bette Midler*

Success can be measured more by obstacles overcome when trying to reach success than by plateaus achieved.

Success is not how high and fast you reach the top, but how high and fast you bounce back when you hit the bottom.

Becoming number one is easier than staying number one.

>—*Senator Bill Bradley (1943–     )*

Success is relative; the more success, the more relatives.

Victory has a hundred fathers, and defeat is an orphan.

>—*John F. Kennedy (1917–1963)*

## Teachers/Teaching

Nothing that is worth knowing can be taught.

>—*Oscar Wilde (1854–1900)*

I hear and I forget. I see and I remember. I do and I understand.

>—*Chinese proverb*

It is what we are that gets across, not what we try to teach.

142

Teacher's complaint: "Not only is he the worst behaved child in my class, but he has perfect attendance."

Upset when only three of his students had listed all of the 50 states correctly on a quiz, the teacher told the class: "When I was in school, we could name every one of the states off the top of our heads."

"Yeah," cracked a student, "but there were only 13 then."

A master can tell you what he expects of you. A teacher, though, awakens your own expectations.

—*Patricia Neal*, As I Am: An Autobiography *(Simon & Schuster)*

You cannot teach a man anything; you can only help him find it within himself. —*Galileo (1564–1642)*

The art of teaching is the art of assisting discovery.
—*Mark Van Doren (1894–1972)*

It is when the gods hate a man with uncommon abhorrence that they drive him into the profession of a schoolmaster.
—*Seneca (5 B.C.–A.D. 65)*

If a doctor, lawyer, or dentist had 40 people in his office at one time, all of whom had different needs, and some of whom didn't want to be there and were causing trouble, and the doctor, lawyer, or dentist, without assistance, had to treat them all with professional excellence for nine months, then he might have some conception of the classroom teacher's job.

The teacher, whether mother, priest, or schoolmaster, is the real maker of history. —*H. G. Wells (1866–1946)*

## Temptation

There are several good protections against temptation, but the surest is cowardice. —*Mark Twain (1835–1910)*

The devil's boots don't creak. —*Scottish proverb*

The trouble with opportunity is that it only knocks. Temptation kicks the door in.

## Time

*Poor man:* Lord, is it true that to you a thousand years is like a minute?
*Lord:* Yes, that's true.
*Poor man:* And is it also true that to you a thousand dollars is like a cent?
*Lord:* Yes, that's so.
*Poor man:* Then, Lord, could you give me a thousand dollars?
*Lord:* Yes, in a minute.

Time wounds all heels.

No great thing is created suddenly, any more than a bunch of grapes or a fig. If you tell me that you desire a fig, I answer you that there must be time. Let it first bloom, then bear fruit, then ripen.
— *Epictetus (ca. A.D. 60)*

Now is the time that people will refer to years from now when they say "in the good old days. . . ."

The less one has to do, the less time one finds to do it in.
— *Lord Chesterfield (1694–1773)*

Thirty days hath September, April, June and November. All the rest have 31, except for January and February, which have 80.

Let every man be master of his time, Till seven at night.
— *William Shakespeare (1564–1616)*

Time may be a great healer, but it's a terrible make-up artist.

Our lives are either spent in doing nothing at all, or in doing nothing to the purpose, or in doing nothing that we ought to do. We are always complaining that our days are few, and acting as though there would be no end to them.
— *Seneca (5 B.C.–A.D. 65)*

Another way to look at life is to look at it as a different kind of department store or shopping mall, where such things as worldly success, love of music, enjoyment of painting, a six-handicap golf game, a close relationship with your daughter, and many other similar things are for sale. But the commodity with which they are purchased is not money but time. And quite contrary to the way the capitalist system works with money and goods, every one of us is given exactly the same amount of time in each hour, and in each day, and in each year. It is a limited amount, and it is impossible for anyone to be so rich in "time" that he can enjoy every single one of the things which time may buy. So there is a choice to be made, just as in purchasing goods with money, although the choice in the one case is far less obvious than the choice in the other.
— *William Rehnquist, Chief Justice, U.S. Supreme Court*

Time is the most valuable thing a man can spend.

—*Diogenes (ca. 320 B.C.)*

## Travel

There ain't no surer way to find out whether you like people or hate them than to travel with them.

—*Mark Twain (1835–1910)*

I'm a public speaker who travels extensively, and ordering room service is part of my usual routine. One morning I awoke, picked up the phone and dialed the operator. "Please connect me with room service," I groggily requested.

"You'll have to dial information, sir."

"Look, I'm tired and hungry," I said in my most authoritative voice. "All I want you to do is connect me to room service."

"Yes, sir, I can tell that you're tired," the operator patiently replied. "But if you'll turn on your light, you'll probably find that you are at home." I did and she was right.

—*Thomas H. Justin*, Reader's Digest

*Reprinted with permission from the August 1989* Reader's Digest. *Copyright © 1989 by The Reader's Digest Assn., Inc.*

It is easier to find a traveling companion than to get rid of one.

With a loaded down station wagon on a family vacation, the father of his troupe finally gave up trying to find Bar Harbor, Maine, and reluctantly pulled up to a man working in his fields along the road. "Excuse me, sir," said the traveler. "Could you tell us if we're a long way from Bar Harbor?"

"Yup," was the response.

"How far?"

147

The farmer thought for a moment and replied, "About 25,000 miles the way you're going, and I don't know how you're going to get over all that water."

—*Nancy Griffin in* Boston

In America, there are two classes of travel—first class, and with children. —*Robert Benchley (1889–1945)*

When traveling by car, the general rule is that the shortest distance between two points is under construction.

Always remember that we pass this way but once. Unless your spouse is reading the road map. —*Robert Orben*

## Truth

No man is so thoroughly right as to be entitled to say that others are totally wrong. It is well to affirm your own truth, but it is not well to condemn those who think differently.

—*Socrates (470–399 B.C.)*

When in doubt, tell the truth. —*Mark Twain (1835–1910)*

One of the most striking differences between a cat and a lie is that a cat has only nine lives. —*Mark Twain (1835–1910)*

Truth is tough. It will not break, like a bubble, at the touch. Nay, you can kick it about all day, and it will be round and full at evening. —*Oliver Wendell Holmes, Sr. (1809–1894)*

To be persuasive, we must be believable; to be believable, we must be credible; to be credible, we must be truthful.

—*Edward R. Murrow (1908–1965)*

Today I bent the truth to be kind, and I have no regret, for I am far surer of what is kind than I am of what is true.

Familiarity breeds contempt. How accurate that is. The reason we hold truth in such respect is because we have so little opportunity to get familiar with it.

—*Mark Twain (1835–1910)*

148

Truth is mighty and will prevail. There is nothing the matter with this, except that it ain't so. —*Mark Twain (1835–1910)*

The truth is found when men are free to pursue it.
—*Franklin D. Roosevelt (1882–1945)*

Man will occasionally stumble over the truth, but most of the time, he will pick himself up and continue on.
—*Winston Churchill (1874–1965)*

As scarce as truth is, the supply has always been in excess of the demand. —*Josh Billings (1818–1885)*

If you tell the truth, you don't have to remember anything.
—*Mark Twain (1835–1910)*

I never give them hell. I just tell the truth and they think it's hell. —*Harry S Truman (1884–1972)*

Every truth passes through three stages before it is recognized. In the first it is ridiculed, in the second it is opposed, and in the third it is regarded as self-evident.

—*Arthur Schopenhauer (1788–1860)*

It has always been desirable to tell the truth, but seldom if ever necessary.                                    —*A. J. Balfour (1848–1930)*

A supervisor wrote on an evaluation form for an employee, "He came to work drunk today." The employee was angry when he saw it, but his supervisor reminded him that one must always state exactly the truth on an evaluation form. When the employee got to fill out his remarks on the evaluation form the next day, he wrote, "My supervisor came to work sober today."

# Virtues

Man sees your actions, but God sees your motives.

—*Thomas à Kempis (1379–1471)*

To be good is noble, but to teach others to be good is even nobler—and less trouble.        —*Mark Twain (1835–1910)*

Many wish not so much to be virtuous, as to seem to be.

—*Cicero (106–43 B.C.)*

Unto the pure, all things are pure.            —*Titus 1:15*

The mind is a like a clock that is constantly running down; it has to be wound up daily with good thoughts.

—*Bishop Fulton J. Sheen (1895–1979)*

It has been my experience that folks who have no vices have very few virtues.        —*Abraham Lincoln (1809–1865)*

It is one of the most beautiful compensations of life that no man can sincerely try to help another without helping himself.

—*Ralph Waldo Emerson (1803–1882)*

Virtue can have naught to do with ease—it craves a steep and thorny path. —*Montaigne (1533–1592)*

There may be said to be two classes of people in the world: those who constantly divide the people of the world into two classes, and those who do not.

—*Robert Benchley (1889–1945)*

I do not pity the unfortunate poor who are in need of charity. I can help them. My heart goes out for the presumably fortunate rich who are not charitable. Nobody can help them.

—*Salem N. Baskin*

Charity will probably remain one of the fine, selfless, human virtues as long as it's tax deductible.

Two men died and waited at the Pearly Gates for admission into heaven. "We've got room for only one more," Saint Peter declared. "Which one of you is more humble?"

The really tough thing about true humility is you can't brag about it.

Hell is paved with good intentions, not bad ones. All men mean well.                                                —*George Bernard Shaw (1856–1950)*

He has all the virtues I dislike and none of the vices I admire.
                                                —*Winston Churchill (1874–1965)*

# War

Only 8 percent of the time since the beginnings of recorded history has the world spent entirely at peace. In 3,521 years, only 256 have been warless. Eight thousand treaties have been broken in this time.                                —Sunshine Magazine

War would end if the dead could return.
  —*Stanley Baldwin, former Prime Minister of Great Britain*

In war, there are no unwounded soldiers.

War hath no fury like a non-combatant.        —*E.C. Montague*

War does not determine who is right—only who is left.

There are no atheists in foxholes.
                                                —*William Thomas Cummings*

What millions died—that Caesar might be great!
                                                —*Thomas Campbell (1777–1844)*

# Winning

It's not true that nice guys finish last. Nice guys are winners before the game even starts.

Winning is a habit. Unfortunately, so is losing.
> —*Vince Lombardi (1913–1970)*

Most people attribute the saying "Winning isn't everything—it's the only thing" to Vince Lombardi, fabled coach of the Green Bay Packers. As Lombardi tried to clarify on numerous occasions, what he really said was, "Winning isn't everything, but wanting to win is."

Win without boasting. Lose without excuse.
> —*Albert Payson Terhune (1872–1942)*

If you cannot win, make the one ahead of you break the record.

# Wisdom

Wise men learn from others' mistakes, fools by their own.

A wise man knows everything; a shrewd one, everybody.

There is somebody wiser than any of us, and that is everybody.
> —*Napoleon Bonaparte (1769–1821)*

Wisdom can never be communicated. It has to be experienced.

Much wisdom can be crowded into four words:
  In God we trust.
  This, too, shall pass.
  Live and let live.
  Still waters run deep.
  Bad news travels fast.
  Nothing succeeds like success.
  Charity begins at home.
  Politics makes strange bedfellows.
  Nothing ventured, nothing gained.
  Man proposes, God disposes.
  Let sleeping dogs lie.

A wise man sees as much as he ought, not as much as he can.
> —*Montaigne (1533–1592)*

Never mistake knowledge for wisdom. One helps you make a living; the other helps you make a life.

No man can be wise on an empty stomach.

—*George Eliot (1819–1880)*

Intelligence is when you find a mistake in your boss's work. Wisdom is when you think about it and decide not to mention it.

The simple realization that there are other points of view is the beginning of wisdom. Understanding what they are is a great step. The final test is understanding *why* they are held.

—*Charles M. Campbell*

154

# Women

The existence of bad women is, and has always been, due to the existence of good women.

—*Menenius Agrippa (ca. 494 B.C.)*

The reason God made woman *after* He made man was that He didn't want any advice.

Nature has given women so much power that the law has very wisely given them little.  —*Samuel Johnson (1709–1784)*

Being powerful is like being a lady. If you have to tell people you are, you aren't.  —*Margaret Thatcher (1925–  )*

The great question that has never been answered, and which I have not yet been able to answer despite my thirty years of research into the feminine soul, is: What does a woman want?

—*Sigmund Freud (1856–1939)*

Whether women are better than men I cannot say—but I can say they are certainly no worse.

—*Golda Meir, former Prime Minister of Israel (1898–1978)*

# Work

The brain is an organ that starts working the moment you get up in the morning and does not stop until you get into the office.  —*Robert Frost (1874–1963)*

Einstein's Three Rules of Work:
1.  Out of clutter find simplicity.
2.  From discord make harmony.
3.  In the middle of difficulty lies opportunity.

*Work.* . . . The job you save may be your own.

The highest reward for a man's toil is not what he gets for it, but rather what he becomes by it.

Any jackass can kick down a barn, but it takes a good carpenter to build one.  —*Sam Rayburn (1882–1961)*

One chops the wood, the other does the grunting.
*—Yiddish proverb*

Don't be so concerned about making a living that you don't take the time to make a life.

The only job in which you start at the top is digging a hole.

Don't go around saying the world owes you a living. . . . It owes you nothing. It was here first.
*—Mark Twain (1835–1910)*

Take your work seriously but yourself lightly.

On a tour of our office, a visitor asked our manager, "How many people work here?"
    The manager replied, "About half."

156

Ergasiophobia—a morbid aversion to any work.

The virtues of hard work are extolled most loudly by people without calluses.

It is not doing the thing we like to do, but liking the thing we have to do, that makes life blessed.

—*Johann Wolfgang von Goethe (1794–1832)*

The biggest mistake you can make is to believe you're working for someone else.

God gave man work, not to burden him, but to bless him, and useful work, willingly, cheerfully, effectively done, has always been the finest expression of the human spirit.

If a man will not work, he shall not eat.

—*II Thessalonians 3:10*

Anyone can do any amount of work, provided it isn't the work he is supposed to be doing at the moment.

—*Robert Benchley (1889–1945)*

"I'm planning a salary increase for you," the boss told the employee.
   "When does it become effective?"
   "Just as soon as you do."

Pray as if everything depended on God, and work as if everything depended on man.

—*Francis Cardinal Spellman (1889–1967)*


# Youth

Youth loves honor and victory more than money.

—*Aristotle (384–322 B.C.)*

The desires of youth show the future virtues of man.

—*Cicero (106–43 B.C.)*

Even if the world progresses generally, youth will always be at the beginning. —*Johann Wolfgang von Goethe (1794–1832)*

How beautiful is youth . . . with its illusions, aspirations, and dreams! —*Henry Wadsworth Longfellow (1807–1882)*

Corruption, vice and laxity are the rule today. This is particularly true among our youth. Our society cannot endure, for the young men of our race are given up unto vain pleasures. They think not of the morrow. They live in folly for the day. Woe, woe to our land, the land of our fathers.

—*Urukagina, ruler of the Sumerians, 2545 B.C.*

# Index